# How to Pray
# in Public
# and at Home

## by T. H. (Tom) Tarbet

HOW TO PRAY IN PRIVATE

HOW TO LEAD IN PUBLIC PRAYER

HOW TO WORK OUT THE WORDING OF A PRAYER

HOW TO PRAY A PRAYER THAT WILL BE
ANSWERED

DEDICATED

to the memory of my parents

the late Tom Sr. and Flossie Tarbet

whose prayers followed me all the days of their lives.

ISBN 0-940999-35-8

**Star Bible Publications**
Fort Worth, Texas 76182

# CONTENTS

*continued* →

Second Printing 1994

First Printing 1988

# CHAPTER ONE
## Use This Book to Open Up An Avenue of Power in Your Life

The first question that comes to your mind is not, "Is this a practical and helpful book?" That's the second question. First you are asking, "Is this book for me?" Answer: It was written with you in mind. It is for everybody who is interested in praying. It is for men and women; for young and old.

### Uppermost

Uppermost in the author's mind is to teach people to lead in prayer. This is not the only purpose, however. Furthermore, one cannot do well as a prayer leader if he does not know how to pray privately.

The author is concerned first to teach the beginner; then all others who want to improve their praying, whether it be praying in public or at home.

### A Self-Help

For a long while I have felt the need for something practical to put into the hands of new converts, as a self-help, that they might learn how to pray and to lead in prayer.

### In Public and at Home

Perhaps the phrases, "in public" and "at home" need to be explained. You pray in public when you are in a meeting of some kind, and you lead in prayer. This is not the only time you pray in public, however. The prayer leader is not the only one who prays. At least, he is not supposed to be. When another leads in prayer and you pray with him in your thoughts and under your breath, you are praying in public. You are participating in a public prayer. Thus in this book we deal with both *(1)* how to lead in prayer and *(2)* how to participate in a prayer led by another.

Then there is praying at home. You do this when you pray with your family. Also, the phrase "at home" is used here to include all your personal prayers when you are alone.

## The Importance of Learning to Pray

"The older I get, the more I see the value of prayer," my father used to say. I now say the same thing. You, too, will come to appreciate more and more the privilege of prayer as the years go rolling by.

"Lord, teach us to pray" was a request made by one of the Lord's disciples (Luke 11:1). The Lord did teach his disciples; for learning how to pray is important. Here are some of the reasons why it is important:

*1.* You need to communicate with your Father who is in Heaven. Once there was a father and son who went on a journey together. The son did not speak to his father one time throughout the long journey. This made the father's heart very sad, for he loved his son. He talked to the boy. He requested the son to talk, but the boy did not say a word. Some Christians are like this boy. I assume you are a Christian. If so, God is your Father. You are his child. He loves you. He is talking to you as you journey through life. The Father talks to you when you read the Bible and when you hear it preached. You talk to him when you pray. Your Father wants you to talk to him and has requested many times in the Bible that you do so.

Doesn't this make it important that you learn how to pray?

*2.* Praise and thanksgiving are to be offered to the Lord. As you know, the Lord deserves your praise. He is worthy of it. "Thou art worthy, O Lord, to receive glory and honor and power: for thou hast created all things, and for thy pleasure they are created" (Revelation 4:11). "And be ye thankful." "Continue in prayer, and watch in the same with thanksgiving." "Giving thanks unto the Father." "Abounding . . . with thanksgiving." These are statements from Paul's letter to the Colossians. Every good and every perfect gift is from God, and you don't want to enjoy all his blessings without expressing thanks. You do not want to be an ingrate.

You are dependent on the Lord for your daily food (Matthew 6:11); and you don't want to be like the pig who gobbles up the acorns on the ground without looking up to the oak from whence they fell. When Jesus fed the 5,000 and later the 4,000, he offered thanks to the Father. Paul said that God created meats for us to receive with thanksgiving and added, "Nothing is to be refused, if it be received with thanksgiving; for it is sanctified by the word of God and prayer" (1 Timothy 4:3-5). For this reason you want to know how to offer grace at the dinner table.

It is more than food. Much more. In the Lord we "live, move and have our being." He gives "to all life, breath and all things" (Acts 17:25,28). Count your many blessings and give thanks.

*3.* Prayer is important to you for another reason. "Your enemy, the devil, as a roaring lion, walketh about, seeking whom he may devour" (1 Peter 5:8). As Jesus said to Peter and the other disciples, "Watch and pray, that ye enter not into temptation: the spirit indeed is willing, but the flesh is weak" (Matthew 26:41). You cannot expect to win your moral and spiritual battles without the Lord's help. It is not easy to live the Christian life, but no disciple ever yielded to Satan while on his knees in prayer. The need for prayer is real. Through prayer you can find power to win.

4. You have the need for daily forgiveness. Forgiveness to the child of God comes through repentance and prayer. "Repent therefore of this thy wickedness, and pray God, if perhaps the thought of thine heart may be forgiven thee" (Acts 8:22). Your need for pardon is very real, for every Christian sins. "If we say that we have no sin, we deceive ourselves, and the truth is not in us" (1 John 1:8). Through repentance and prayer you can get rid of the guilt feeling by getting rid of the guilt.

5. You have many other needs, both temporal and spiritual; and it is up to you to ask for them. "Ask, and it shall be given you . . . ." (Matthew 7:7). "Ye have not, because ye ask not" (James 4:2b). You need the Lord's blessings. We all do. Jesus declared, "Without me ye can do nothing" (John 15:5b). Of course you want to pray. If you don't know how, you want to learn. If you already know how, you want to learn to pray better.

6. Also, there are others who need your prayers. "The effectual, fervent prayer of a righteous man availeth much" (James 5:16b). You want to give others the benefit of your prayers. There will be times when members of your family will be ill or in trouble. Other people, too. They will need your prayers. There is much suffering in this old world. Your prayers can help to bring about changes. The English have the right idea when they include in their prayers, a request for God's blessings upon "those who are distressed at sea," and when they ask for "journeying mercies" for those who are traveling.

All men need your prayers. Some of those who do are our political leaders. "I exhort therefore, that, first of all, supplications, prayers, intercessions, and giving of thanks, be made for all men; for kings, and all that are in authority; that we may lead a quiet and peaceable life in all godliness and honesty" (1 Timothy 2:1,2). Help to bring about better government and a better world through your prayers. In Romans 10:1-3, Paul prayed for lost sinners. You and I need to do the same. Since men are saved by the gospel and must obey the gospel (1 Corinthians 15:1-3; 2 Thessalonians 1:8), we cannot ask God to save people in their disobedience; but you and I can pray for those who are preaching the gospel throughout the community, the nation and the world. We can pray that lost people may hear and obey. Help make soul-winning efforts more effective: Pray.

Pray for more workers to be sent out. "Then saith he unto his disciples, 'The harvest truly is plenteous, but the labourers are few; pray ye therefore the Lord of harvest, that he will send forth labourers into his harvest'" (Matthew 9:37,38).

The apostle Paul felt a need for the prayers of his brethren, and requested them (Ephesians 6:18,19, et al).

Make a prayer list; a list of people and things you want to mention in intercessory prayer. Here is suggested list: *(1)* your home congregation and *(2)* the Lord's church everywhere. *(3)* gospel preachers; especially your local preacher, and those who have gone out to far away and difficult places. *(4)* your congregational leaders and other members. *(5)* people lost in sin; especially certain ones you are trying to lead to Christ. *(6)* your nation and her leaders, and all the world leaders, that we may lead quiet and peaceable lives in all godliness and gravity. *(7)* sick people; those you know and others. *(8)* your companion. *(9)* each child. *(10)* each grandchild. *(11)* parents. *(12)* grandparents, and *(13)* your enemies (Matthew 5:44).

"Men ought always to pray," Jesus said (Luke 18:1). It's important to pray. It's important to learn how. Prayer can be an avenue of power in your life.

*7.* You need to pray with your brothers in Christ. There is added value in united prayer. When persecution first came to the church, the disciples lifted up their voice with one accord in prayer. The early disciples prayed together in their assemblies; and the Lord promises to be present with you when two or three are come together in his name. See Acts 4:21-30; Matthew 18:20; 1 Corinthians 14:15,16.

Christians are admonished to not forsake the assembling of themselves together (Hebrews 10:25); and all should come as participants in the worship; not as spectators. You should come to pray with others; not just to listen to someone else pray. There's power in united prayer.

*8.* Learn how to lead in prayer, too. Someone must take the lead. Why should it be someone else? You may not be a preacher. Your work may be something different. But if you are a Christian, you are a priest in the temple of God, the church. John was writing to the seven congregations in Asia (not just to their preachers) when he said the Lord "hath made us kings and priests unto God" (Revelation 1:4-6a). So every Christian is a priest. There is no special priesthood in the Lord's church. There was in the Old Testament church, but it had a typical meaning. There was one man who was high priest, and there were many who were common priests. The priests were the ones qualified to preside at the worship of the tabernacle, and later, the temple. Only the high priest could enter the "holy of holies" with blood and make the atonement. In the fulfillment of this type today, Christ is the high priest (Hebrews 5:8-10), and as we have seen, all Christians are priests. There can be no special priesthood among the members of the church, for the only person above the common priests is that of the high priest. No man can be high priest, for that office belongs to Christ alone. Therefore, all Christians are common priests. All are alike. There's no "clergy" class which stands between the people and Christ.

For one thing, this means that all Christians are qualified to offer their own worship. No one has to look to a special minister to offer his worship for him. It also means that all are qualified to preside in a service of worship. Allowance must be made for the fact that women are not to be the leaders (I Timothy 2:11-15). This restriction has to do with their relation to men. This restriction does not apply in a service where men are not present. Women are free to preside in Bible classes of women and children and even in Sunday communion services where only women are present. Under such circumstances, women can lead the prayers and do whatever else needs to be done.

When Wanna (my first wife) was a small girl in Melrose, New Mexico, the church was very small and weak. At one time only a group of women were in attendance. No men came; not even on Sunday. The sisters had it all to do. They taught classes, led the prayers and presided at the Lord's table. They had every right to do so under the circumstances. It's a good thing these Melrose sisters knew how, and were willing to undertake this work. Had they not, the church there would have died.

Women, as well as men, need to learn to lead in prayer. Women will need to lead prayers in ladies' Bible classes and in children's classes which they teach. They will need to pray with their children at home and to teach their children to pray. Let the women learn how to pray too.

Surely, it is agreed that all Christian men need to know how to lead in prayer. Besides leading prayer at home, you will need to help teach your children to pray. Indeed there are many reasons for learning to pray and to lead in prayer.

So, learn to pray. Learn how to pray in public and at home. It will be a blessing to others. It will be a help to the church.

## *How to Make Good Use of this Book*

For one thing, this book can be used in class teaching as a help, with the Bible as the text. Two of the longer chapters are sub-divided into sections, so that one class period can be spent on each section. The book naturally lends itself to a thirteen lesson study. A qualified Bible teacher will have no problem presenting the class with questions and making assignments.

The first design of the book is to help the individual as he teaches himself how to pray. Take your Bible and this book and learn how. You can do it. Here are some suggestions as to how:

First, read with a pencil in hand. Underscore points and sections that especially impress you. Also make check marks at the beginning of key sentences. Mark sparingly at first.

Having read through the book once, start again at the first and study it by lessons, completing the exercise at the end of each lesson. A chapter is one lesson, except in the cases where chapters are subdivided into sections. In those cases, one section is usually a lesson.

Start immediately putting into practice what you have learned. You learn to do by doing. As you try to put into practice what you have learned, pick up the book periodically to check on what you are doing.

Anytime you read the book it is wise to make comments at the top or bottom of the pages or in the margins. Also in the flyleaves. Don't hesitate to mark up your book; but be conservative. If you mark every page it will take you as long to read your markings as to re-read the book.

Re-read the book a third time within a month or six weeks.

After that you may need to review certain chapters or sections.

Keep the book on the table by your reading lamp, where you will be reminded to review certain portions of it from time to time, for you want to continue to improve your praying and your prayer leading.

Don't forget to ask the Lord to help you as you study and practice praying.

In other words: *(1)* Read the book through, *(2)* Then study chapter by chapter, doing the exercises, *(3)* Review the book within four to six weeks, *(4)* Keep the book by your reading lamp and review parts of it periodically, *(5)* Finally, remember to ask God to help you in your study. He will.

## A Quotation

I end this chapter with some striking words taken from the Gospel Advocate of February 24, 1944:

The problems of this complicated world have driven men of all ages and places to seek the guidance of some higher power. There is a childlike feeling of loneliness and helplessness in the heart of nearly every human being. Behind the confident front that men put up there is a longing for support and strength that only God can give. The literature of all nations has revealed that this attitude is characteristic of all mankind.

The initial way in which this yearning for help discloses itself is in prayer. Abraham Lincoln expressed the sentiment of numberless care-weary, toilworn souls when he said: "I have been driven many times to my knees by the overwhelming conviction that I had nowhere else to go; my wisdom and all that was around me seemed insufficient for the day . . . ."

It is highly important to teach men how to pray that their prayers may be acceptable to the Almighty. That is evidently the purpose of the request which the disciples of Jesus made of him: "Lord, teach us to pray, as John also taught his disciples." They already felt intensely the need of prayer. They recognized the power of prayer in the life of their Master and were anxious to learn how to effectively reach the Father's throne of mercy and grace.

Prayer has the power to open the door to the inexhaustible treasure house of God's eternal goodness.

Like these disciples long ago, may we approach the study of prayer with the request on our lips and in our hearts: "Lord, teach us to pray."

## Exercise

1.   Take the eight reasons given for learning to pray and on a sheet of paper list them in order of their importance to you.

2.   Did John the Baptist teach his disciples to pray? Give Bible reference.

3.   On a separate sheet of paper make out your own prayer list. What item of importance was omitted from the prayer list in this book, according to Matthew?

### Footnote on Women Leading in Prayer Where Men are Present

In woman's relation to man she is not to teach in a position of authority. This is the import of 1 Timothy 2:11-12. "Let a woman learn in quietness with all subjection. But Permit not a woman to teach, nor to have dominion over a man, but to be in quietness" (ASV).

Just above this statement, and in harmony with it, the apostle distinguishes between men and women in the matter of prayer. "I will therefore that men pray everywhere . . . . In like manner also that women adorn themselves in modest apparel . . . ." The Greek words *"tous andras"* were used when Paul said "that men pray everywhere." This is used in contrast with women (Gr. *gunaikas"*) in the next verse. In other words, men, as distinct from women, are to pray everywhere. The word for men, *"andras"* is from *"anar."* The normal meaning of this word is "a male person of full age and stature, as opposed to a child or female." See Harper's Analytical Greek Lexicon; also Thayer. This is certainly the idea here, as seen from the way this word is set off from the word for women: "that men pray everywhere . . . that women adorn themselves in modest apparel." One can tell from the English versions that men and women are set in contrast to one another in this passage.

The context of this scripture shows the writer is speaking of the public worship, which was attended by both men and women.

Another thing: There's a teaching quality to prayer. The prayer leader teaches. If a woman leads a group in prayer, she is leading in a teaching situation. Note John 11:41,32: ". . . And Jesus lifted up his eyes, and said, Father, I thank thee that thou hearest me. And I know that thou hearest me always: but because of the multitude that stand by I said it, that they may believe that thou hast sent me." His prayer had a teaching value. If then, one believes a woman's work is not of preaching the sermon or handling the Bible class where men are present, how can he believe that she should lead in prayer when men are in the same group?

None of this means that women are inferior. It means they are different from men. Having made them different, God gave men and women different roles. Woman's submission to man is a principle grounded in creation, as per 1 Timothy 2:11-15. It is not to be explained away as something which was only established by custom.

# CHAPTER TWO

## How to Pray a Prayer
## That Will Be Answered

"I believe in prayer because prayer has produced results. Some people say there is nothing in it . . . . That only means they, themselves, have found nothing. A blind man will say he does not see a mountain. An unsuccessful prospector will declare there is no gold in such and such a stream. But the mountain and the gold are both there."

Dr. Daniel Poling

D avid once addressed God in these words, "O thou that hearest prayer, unto thee shall all flesh come" (Psalms 65:2). God answers prayer.

There are some prayers, however, which he does not answer. Notice the following statements from Scripture: "And the Lord will not hear you in that day," "And when ye spread forth your hands, I will hide mine eyes from you: yea, when ye make many prayers, I will not hear," "Let not that man think he shall receive anything of the Lord" (1 Samuel 8:18; Isaiah 1:15; James 1:7).

## Conditions to Acceptable Praying

The posture of the body is not one of the conditions, except in as far as one's posture may indicate his attitude toward God, such as reverence or irreverence. We find in the Bible that men of both testaments prayed from various postures. Hannah "stood" by the priest, Eli, praying (1 Samuel 1:26) and the Lord heard her. Jesus said, "When ye stand praying, forgive . . . ." (Mark 11:25).

The Lord prayed in both a kneeling and a prostrate position in Gethsemane (Luke 22:41; Matthew 26:39). The Apostle instructed men to "pray everywhere, lifting up holy hands" (1 Timothy 2:8). On one occasion we find people praying with lifted hands and bowed heads (Nehemiah 8:6). Jonah "prayed unto the Lord his God out of the fish's belly" (Jonah 2:1). King David sat down and prayed, according to 1 Chronicles 17:16.

One editor of a religious journal severely criticized the church for praying while seated in the pews. He said it is irreverent. To be consistent he should also object to the congregation singing while seated; for many of the hymns are prayers. Jonah couldn't have stood to pray in the fish's belly; and often in the assembly we have people who are scarcely able to stand. If people are to be continuously conscious of the Lord's presence and live in a prayerful mood, they are likely to do some praying while lying in bed at night.

On the other hand, it is proper for us to speak out against laziness on the part of worshippers and on behalf of a better expression of reverence.

Posture within itself is not the concern. There are things, however, which must be observed if your prayer is to be answered.

*1.* You must pray with reverence and humility. " . . . Whereby we may serve God acceptably with reverence and godly fear: for our God is a consuming fire" (Hebrews 12: 28,29). "Humble yourselves in the sight of the Lord . . . " (James 4:10). This has always been true. Long ago Micah said, "He hath showed thee, O man, what is good; and what doth the Lord require of thee, but to do justly, and to love mercy, and to walk humbly with thy God" (Micah 6:8).

When it comes to the attitude of prayer, reverence and humility are key words. Remember the humility of the publican in Luke 18.

*2.* Sincerity and simplicity are essentials. Prayer is the sincere desire of the heart, expressed to God and designed to please him rather than the people who may be listening. The Lord's instructions are, "And when thou prayest, thou shalt not be as the hypocrites are: for they love to pray standing in the synagogues and in the corners of the streets, that they may be seen by men. Verily I say unto you, they have their reward" (Matthew 6:5). In the same connection Jesus said to not use vain repetitions in your prayers. Then he gave a simple little prayer as a model for his disciples.

If one is not sincere, he is nothing. And sincerity naturally expresses itself in simplicity.

James B. Miner points out that one should not pray like this:

> We respectfully petition, request and entreat that due and adequate provision be made, this day and the date hereinafter prescribed, for the satisfying of this petitioner's nutritional requirements and for the organizing of such methods as may be deemed necessary and proper to assure the reception by and for said petitioner of such quantities of baked cereal products as shall, in the judgement of the aforesaid petitioner, constitute a sufficient supply thereof.

Translation: "Give us this day our daily bread."

Keep it simple, my sincere brother.

*3.* Pray unselfishly. A Christian is basically unselfish; as is Christ, his great example. This Christian attitude is to be reflected even in our prayers. "You ask and do not receive, because you ask with wrong motives, so that you may spend it in your pleasures" (James 4:3, NASV).

Jesus didn't teach us to pray, "Give me my daily bread," but, "Give us our daily bread."

> Lord, help me to live from day to day
>
> In such a self forgetting way
>
> That even when I kneel to pray,
>
> My prayer may be for others.
>
> -C.D. Meigs

This doesn't mean you can't ask for legitimate needs for yourself. You are invited to ask for these things (James 4:2). Yet you can be unselfish in your prayers. You need to be if you want them to be answered.

*4.* Pray out of a grateful heart. "In everything by prayer and supplication, with thanksgiving, let your requests be made known unto God" (Philippians 4:6). " . . . and be ye thankful" (Colossians 3:15). "Abounding therein with thanksgiving" (Colossians 2:7b).

Thanksgiving should occupy a large place in a person's prayers. I admire the uneducated railroad worker, who lived in Richmond, Virginia many years ago. At noon he would take a New Testament from his lunch pail and read from it. Some of the other workers teased him. One day a man said to him, "Sam, you must be very religious. Tell me, do you pray a lot?" Sam answered, "Yess'r, I do." This response brought another question: "Sam, what do you ask the Lord to give you when you pray?" Sam's answer: "I don't ask him to give me noth'n; I just thanks him for what he has already given me."

Sometimes when Jesus prayed he just gave thanks for something and made no petition (Matthew 11:25, 26; John 11:41, 42.

Certainly there are things you need to request of the Lord; but mostly, if you will express your gratitude for the many, many things he has given you, your other needs will be taken care of. The Lord delights in blessing those who are grateful. "Bless the Lord, O my soul, and forget not all his benefits" (Psalms 103:2).

5. Pray fervently. Pray with earnestness. "The effectual fervent prayer of a righteous man availeth much" (James 5:16b). It is said of Christ, when he was in the garden, "And being in an agony, he prayed more earnestly" (Luke 22:44a). It is said of him in Hebrews 5:7 that he offered up "Prayers and supplications with strong cries and tears." When Paul wrote his letter to the Colossians, Epaphras was "laboring fervently" for them in prayers (Colossians 4:12).

In keeping with fervency, another condition to acceptable praying is:

6. Importunity. Be persistent. Pray repeatedly. Don't give up and quit asking because you don't receive an answer promptly. As someone has said, God has three answers to prayer: Yes, No, and Wait awhile.

If you have reason to believe your request is in keeping with God's will, then keep praying for it. "Continue in prayer" (Colossians 4:2a), "Continuing instant in prayer" (Romans 12:12c). When Peter was held in prison in Jerusalem, "prayer was made without ceasing of the church unto God for him" (Acts 12:5b). See also Luke 11:5-10.

It may be this is the reason some of your prayers remain unanswered. It may be you gave up too quickly.

7. Pray in faith. The inspired writer made a definite promise when he said. "If any of you lack wisdom, let him ask of God, that giveth to all men liberally, and upbraideth

not, and it shall be given him." However, he was quick to add these words, "Let him ask in faith, nothing wavering. For he that wavereth is like a wave of the sea driven with the wind and tossed. For let not that man think that he shall receive anything of the Lord" (James 1:5-7).

You have to trust. Don't be like the farmer, who, during a time of drought went to the community center to join in the prayers for rain. He was asked to lead one of the prayers. In his fervency, he didn't just request that the drought be broken, but he asked God to send a "gulley washer." On his way home after the prayer meeting he was caught in a flash flood and nearly drowned. He was also caught by surprise. Had he really thought the Lord would answer his prayer, he would not have requested a "gulley washer." I don't know whether the hard rain that night came in answer to prayer; but if so, it was not this man's prayer. He did not ask in faith.

If you want your prayer answered, ask in faith. "Believe that ye receive and ye shall have" (Mark 11:24 lit.)

*8.* Pray as a righteous man. If you are not already that way, become righteous. It is the "effectual fervent prayer of a righteous man that availeth much" (James 5:16b). "For the eyes of the Lord is against them that do evil" (1 Peter 3:12).

Such Scriptures certainly make it plain that one needs to be righteous to have his prayers answered. The kind of righteousness one needs is "the righteousness which is of God by faith," as Paul said in Philippians 3:9. One may be ever so good morally, and not be righteous in God's sight. One may be religious, even zealously religious, and not be righteous in God's sight. Such was true of the Jews of Paul's day. They were lost, and he prayed for their salvation. He said, "Brethren, my heart's desire and prayer to God for Israel is that they might be saved. For I bear them record that they have a zeal of God, but not according to knowledge. For they being ignorant of God's righteousness, and going about to establish their own righteousness, have not submitted themselves unto the righteousness of God" (Romans 10:1-3). They were lost because they had not submitted to the righteousness of God. The lost man is not righteous, even if he is moral in his behavior and zealously religious.

Therefore, it would not be the "effectual, fervent prayer of a righteous man" unless it was the prayer of a Christian (a saved man). After all, who else would have the right to call God his father? The model prayer, given by our Lord, begins, "Our Father" (Matthew 6:9). Only the child of God can rightly call God, Father; and as Galatians 3:26 states, "For ye are all the children of God by faith in Christ Jesus" (obedient faith, as the next verse makes plain). The unbeliever is not a child of God.

One must become righteous to claim the promise that his prayers will be answered; hence, one must become a Christian. Prayer is a Christian's privilege. God wants all men to pray. He wants all men to pray; but he wants them to become Christians, then pray.

After being made righteous (being converted), one is called on to live righteously. If he doesn't do so his prayers are hindered. To God's children of the Old Covenant, Isaiah wrote, "But your iniquities have separated between you and your God, and your sins have hid his face from you, that he will not hear" (Isaiah 59:2). The New Testament tells us to "lift up holy hands" in prayer (1 Timothy 2:8b).

To live righteously is to live in obedience to God's word, and that's the way to have your prayers answered. As the apostle John said, "And whatsoever we ask, we receive of him, because we keep his commandments, and do those things that are pleasing in his sight" (1 John 3:22).

This involves more than Christian morality. Righteous living includes fruit bearing for Christ. To claim the promise that God will answer your prayer, you must bring forth fruit. Notice what Jesus said, "Ye have not chosen me, but I have chosen you, and ordained you, that ye should go and bring forth fruit, and that your fruit should remain: that whatsoever ye shall ask of the Father in my name, he may give it you" (John 15:16).

That the one praying needs to be a Christian is also evident from condition number 9, which we will take up in section 2 of this chapter.

At this point we stop to review the eight conditions to acceptable praying which we have discussed. The thoughts we have projected are important to you. They need to be chewed well and digested. Review them. Think about them. Look up the references in your Bible. Do the exercise given below.

## *Exercise*

1. Read Luke 18: 9-14, and in your own words, write down what this teaches you about one or more of the conditions of acceptable praying.

2. Do the same with Luke 11:5-10.

3. Which of the eight conditions are most commonly neglected today, in your opinion? List three.

4. Name two specific acts, as given in James 1:26 and 1 Peter 3:7, which cause the prayers of an unrighteous man to be hindered.

# CHAPTER TWO

## How to Pray a Prayer
## That Will Be Answered

### SECTION 2

In the first section of this chapter we learned that God answers prayers, but not all prayers. The Bible gives conditions that must be met by the person praying. We considered eight of them. In this section we will take up four more.

9. Pray in the name of Christ. Coming near the end of the Jewish economy and the beginning of the Christian age, Jesus said to his disciples, "Whatsoever ye shall ask the Father in my name, he will give it you. Hitherto have ye asked nothing in my name: ask, and ye shall receive, that your joy may be full" (John 16: 23b,24). Here again you have a sure promise of the answer to prayer, but it is conditioned upon your asking in Christ's name. See also John 14:13,14; Colossians 3:17.

The Bible doesn't state that you must say the words, "I pray in the name of Jesus Christ." It doesn't specify what you say; but what you do. You pray in his name. You pray by his authority; through him; pleading his merit. It is good to form the habit of stating the prayer is being offered in the Lord's name. Stating it in a public prayer serves to remind everyone that the prayer is being offered in the Lord's name. And why shouldn't you state it, if you are not ashamed of your Lord? I suggest you form the habit of doing this.

Surely it's obvious that only a Christian can pray in the name of Christ. Only he can rightly plead the Lord's merits, approach the Father through Christ and offer a prayer by his authority.

It is necessary that you do all things in his name, giving thanks to God the Father through him, we are told in Colossians 3:17. Pray in his name. It takes his name to give power to your prayers.

*10.* Pray in penitence. The fact that you are righteous doesn't mean you are perfect. No one is. Even John the Apostle of Love wasn't. He included himself in the statement, "If we say we have no sin, we deceive ourselves, and the truth is not in us" (1 John 1:8).

John went on to say, "If we confess our sins, he is faithful and just to forgive us our sins, and to cleanse us from all unrighteousness" (1 John 1:9). In this statement he inferred penitence. In Acts 8:22, the word "repent" is used. An erring Christian is told, "Repent therefore of this thy wickedness, and pray God, if perhaps the thought of thine heart may be forgiven thee." A part of humility is the recognition that one is sinful and unworthy before the Lord. In the model prayer, Jesus included the petition, "Forgive us our debts" (Matthew 6:12). This petition belongs in almost every prayer. Be "Poor in spirit." Don't think of yourself "more highly than you ought to think." Remember, "The sacrifices of God are a broken spirit: a broken and contrite heart, O God, thou wilt not despise" (Psalm 51:17).

I don't know how common this situation is among Christians, but once, when I moved to a Texas town to work with the church, I noticed that the public prayers never included a petition for forgiveness. This went on for weeks. Something had to be wrong. I thought of the parable of the Pharisee and Publican (Luke 18:9-14) and began to preach on humility and penitence in prayer. As a result, these good brethren, like those everywhere I have been, being taught better, did better. They learned to pray in penitence. Everyone must, if his prayers are to be heard.

*11.* Pray with a forgiving attitude. You need forgiveness from God; so you must forgive others. Jesus said, "after this manner therefore pray ye, . . . . forgive us our debts, as we forgive our debtors." He went on to make this comment, "For if ye forgive men their trespasses, your heavenly Father will also forgive you, but if ye forgive not men their trespasses, neither will your Father forgive your trespasses" (Matthew 6:14,15).

No doubt this explains why the prayers of many people are not answered. They have hatred in their hearts, or they hold grudges. They are not willing and ready to forgive everyone his brother "from the heart" (Matthew 18: 35b). Make sure this is not the case with you.

"Let all bitterness, and wrath, and anger, and clamour, and evil speaking, be put away from you, with all malice: and be ye kind one to another, tenderhearted, forgiving one another, even as God for Christ's sake hath forgiven you" (Ephesians 4:31,32).

There's no way to disobey this passage and pray a prayer that will be answered.

*12.* Ask in accordance with God's will, when you pray. Do you have confidence when you pray? If so, is it based on the same thing on which John based his confidence? He said, "And this is the confidence that we have in Him, that, if we ask anything according to his will, he heareth us" (1 John 5:14). In this Scripture we have another promise that prayer will be answered. Again a condition is given: "If we ask anything according to his will."

You have no right to ask the Lord to set aside his will to grant you something you want, as I am sure you agree. One day two Mormon "elders" came to my door for a study. As the talking proceeded one asked if I would be wiling to take the Book of Mormon and read it, asking God to show me whether or not it is true. This is a proposition they often make to people. At first it sounded like a fair proposition. But I had to turn it down because it is wrong to pray for things which are contrary to God's will. God had already told me in the Bible that there are to be no later day revelations. The Christian faith was once delivered to the saints ("once for all," according to the revised versions) as Jude, verse 3 states. All things that pertain to life and godliness "hath been given unto us," Peter said in the first century (2 Peter 1:3b). In other words: No later day revelations from God. This is according to the will of God. Why then should I ask the Lord to reveal to me that which he had already told me in the Bible? Should I tempt God this way? No, I already knew the Book of Mormon was not inspired of God, without reading it. I knew this because I had read the Bible. Thus I could not ask the Lord to show me whether or not the Book of Mormon was his book.

There are many ways in which a prayer may fail to meet this requirement. For example, some preachers instruct the alien sinner to pray for salvation. This is contrary to God's will. Salvation is by faith, and the Bible does not teach that faith comes by prayer, as some seem to think. The Bible says, "So then faith cometh by hearing, and hearing by the word of God" (Romans 10:17). Jesus didn't send his disciples into the lost world to pray for every creature that he might be saved. In sending them out, he said, "Go into all the world, and preach the gospel to every creature; he that believeth and is baptized shall be saved; but he that believeth not shall be damned" (Mark 16: 15,16). Sinners don't purify their souls by "praying through to victory." Salvation comes by an obedient faith. The Bible says, "Seeing ye have purified your souls in obeying the truth through the Spirit unto unfeigned love of the brethren . . . " (1 Peter 1:22). The Book says, "Ye have obeyed from the heart that form of doctrine which was delivered you. Being then made free from sin, ye became the servants of righteousness" (Romans 6:17b,18). Jesus declared, "Not everyone that saith unto me,

Lord, Lord, shall enter into the kingdom of heaven; but he that doeth the will of my Father which is in heaven" (Matthew 7:21). That's the same as saying, not everyone who prays; but he who obeys, shall enter the kingdom of heaven. What could be plainer? It is not according to God's will to pray that the Lord save an alien sinner in his unbelief or disobedience. We can't ask God to set aside his will.

Don't think I'm forgetting that "whosoever shall call on the name of the Lord shall be saved" (Acts 2:21; Romans 10:13). This is not in conflict with what we have just learned. Calling on the Lord, as used in these passages, is not praying through to salvation. Let the Bible explain it. Romans 10 and Acts 2 do not refer to a spoken prayer at all, and do not justify the sinner in praying instead of obeying. Our Lord asked this pertinent question: "And why call ye me, Lord, Lord, and do not the things which I say?" (Luke 6:46). Calling on the name of the lord to be saved is explained in Acts 22:16. In this verse, a believing and penitent man, who did not yet have his sins washed away, was told, "And why tarriest thou? Arise, and be baptized, and wash away thy sins, calling on the name of the Lord." He was to be calling on the name of the Lord in his baptism ("be baptized . . . calling on the name of the Lord"). If this refers to making a prayer, it is to be made while one is being baptized; and that is not what modern preachers mean when they tell sinners to pray through to salvation before, and without being baptized. They say baptism has nothing to do with it. But Acts 22:16 connects calling on the name of the Lord with baptism. It should be obvious what is meant here. The man did not yet have his sins washed away in the blood of the Lamb. This needed to be brought about. He was told he could bring it about by being baptized. Not simply by being baptized. He would need to be seeking forgiveness from the Lord. He could not look to the water as the cleansing fount. He would need to look away from the water to the Lord who had shed his blood for the remission of sins. He would need to be calling on the name of the Lord. Trusting in the Lord, and in the Lord alone. He was to express the desire of his heart by being baptized. Jesus had commanded baptism. It is for the forgiveness of sins (Acts 2:38). One must want forgiveness badly enough to submit to the command, and his obedience will be an act of trust in the Lord. It will be an unspoken prayer for forgiveness.

If you have not already done so as a penitent believer, "be baptized and wash away thy sins, calling on the name of the Lord." But don't ask God to set aside his requirements and save you in disobedience. This would not be praying according to God's will.

So far we have discussed matters about which God expressed his will in the Scriptures. In such things you can know God's will before you pray. Besides these things there are other matters about which you cannot know the Lord's will ahead of time. God has not revealed his will in these matters. For instance, you don't know ahead of time whether it is God's will that you move into a certain city, stay a year there and operate a successful business. "Go to now, you that say, today or tomorrow we will go into such a city, and continue there a year, and buy and sell, and get gain. Whereas ye know not what shall be on the morrow . . . For what ye ought to say, if the Lord will, we shall live and do this or that . . . (James 4:13-15). If you are planning to make a move, surely you ought to pray about it. But you can only ask the Lord to bless you in the project, if it is his will. You should include this statement in your petition.

When Jesus prayed that the cup of suffering be removed from him, he added, "Nevertheless, not my will, but thine be done" (Luke 2:42).

This is the way we should pray for the sick. We can surely pray for all the sick: but obviously it is not the Lord's will to heal all the sick. If so, death could be avoided; a thing that cannot be done, according to Hebrews 9:27. When we pray for the sick, we need to ask for their healing if it be the Lord's will.

Our praying for the sick, is not to be confused with the miraculous healing of sick people in Bible times. That had a special purpose in the formative period of the church, and no attempt was made to heal every person. When the attempt was made there were no failures. No one had to go home unhealed. And it was not a matter of the sick person gradually getting better. The healing was always immediate. The promise for those who were to be given the gift of healing was that when they lay hands on the sick, "they shall recover" (Mark 16:18). It was not, "They may recover" or "Some of them shall recover." It was, "They shall recover." As the Lord's healers went out (after this promise was given) we have not a single record of their trying, but failing to heal. So, don't confuse this with the prayers we should make for the sick.

The point is, <u>we must pray for things which are in keeping with God's will, if our prayers are to be answered</u>.

## Summary

To pray a prayer that will be answered, you need to:

1. Pray with reverence and humility

2. Sincerity and simplicity are key words

3. Pray unselfishly

4. From a grateful heart

5. Pray fervently

6. With importunity

7. Pray in faith

8. As a righteous person

9. In the name of Jesus Christ

10. With penitence

11. Have a forgiving attitude

12. Ask in accordance with God's will

## *How to Know When Your Prayers Are Being Answered*

You often hear the statement, "God answered my prayers. I know he did, for I received what I was praying for." But even when the blessing asked for is received, it may not be in answer to your prayer. It definitely is not if you have failed to meet the Bible conditions to acceptable praying.

There are certain factors that often are forgotten. Let us note the possibilities.

*1.* God sends some of his blessings for other reasons than prayer. For example, God's love for all of mankind causes him to send rain on both the just and the unjust (Matthew 5:45). In the case of the unjust, it surely is not because they prayed for rain. Many of them do not pretend to pray. Still the blessing comes. So, God may send one a blessing because of his own love and without consideration of the man's prayers.

*2.* One may receive a blessing, not in answer to his prayers, but in answer to the prayers of someone else. Someone else may have been praying for him. Were this not so, he may not have received the blessing. This possibility must not be ignored.

In both cases, one may know the blessing is from the Lord. Every good and perfect gift is (James 1:17). God should be thanked and praised for the gift. This much we know. But why did he send the blessing? It could possibly have been reason number 1 or reason number 2, as given above. It could be that the person's own prayers were not answered. There's no person whose prayers are responsible for all the blessing she receives. Also, there are evidently people whose prayers are not responsible for any of the blessings they get from God.

3. Yet, it's possible for one to know God is answering his prayers. He can have confidence about it. Note what is said in 1 John 5:14,15, "And this is the confidence which we have in him, that, if we ask anything according to his will, he heareth us: and if we know that he heareth us, whatsoever we ask, we know that we have the petitions that we desire of him."

The praying people under consideration here are Christians. They are righteous people. People who do things in the name of the Lord. People who are humble and penitent when they sin. All this is inferred. The apostle John included himself in the statement by using the personal pronoun, "we." Even then, there was an "if." It was, "If we ask anything according to his will." We cannot be fair and assume that a single one of the conditions to acceptable praying is left out in the cases under consideration. Surely not, for the Scriptures are not self-contradictory. The passage in 1 John 5 does not nullify those verses which name the conditions to acceptable praying.

Actually 1 John 5 is telling people who meet the condition, that they can have confidence their prayers are being answered. Their confidence is based on the promise that God will answer such prayers.

And as one's experiences multiply through the years, he comes to see his prayers answered. He knows he is praying according to God's requirements, and he sees the blessings come time after time. There's no reason to think that all the blessings are coming in answer to someone else's prayers.

His prayers are being answered. But for him to know this, he must know he is praying the Bible way. Complying with the conditions given in the Scriptures. By praying, time after time, the kind of prayer that God answers, he knows his prayers are being heard.

In fact, before the blessings come, he can be sure that God is answering his prayers, as is stated in 1 John 5:14,15.

## *Exercise*

1. Take a sheet of paper, and without looking at the book, write down the 12 conditions to acceptable praying that are given in this chapter. If you can't do it the first time, review the chapter, then close the book and try again. It is not important that you list them in the exact order given in the chapter.

2. Copy out of your Bible one verse in connection with each condition to show that it is a Bible condition.

3. When you have a problem, would it be worth while to request the prayers of just any person, regardless of his religion or personal life? Give Bible reason for your answer.

4. Of whom does the Bible say, "his prayer shall be abomination?"

NOTE: God did answer a prayer made by an unsaved man named Cornelius. He did so by putting this truth-seeker in contact with a gospel preacher, who told him how to be saved. See Acts of Apostles 10:1–5 and 11:12–14. This is in keeping with the promise of John 7:17, "If any man willeth to do his will, he shall know of the teaching. . . ." This is far different from the promise made to God's children in such places as 1 John 3:22, namely, "Whatsoever we ask we receive of him." Review the Scriptures given earlier in this chapter.

# CHAPTER THREE
## The Model Prayer

Y ou, like all of us, will learn from the prayers of others. From prayers you hear. From prayers you read. For this reason it is suggested that you study the various prayers found in the Bible. Not only one time. You will find it helpful to turn and re-read many of these prayers over and over.

The best model is the prayer Jesus gave his disciples. He was teaching them how to pray. He was teaching all of us how to pray. What a privilege it is to have the Master Teacher as your instructor. Sit at his feet and learn how to pray.

This prayer is given, with slight differences, in two places: Luke 11:1-4: "And it came to pass, that as he was praying in a certain place, when he ceased, one of his disciples said unto him, Lord, teach us to pray, as John also taught his disciples. And He said unto them, "When ye pray say: Our Father which art in heaven, Hallowed be thy name. Thy kingdom come. Thy will be done as in heaven, so in earth. Give us day by day our daily bread. And forgive us our sins; for we also forgive everyone that is indebted to us. And lead us not into temptation, but deliver us from evil."

Matthew 6:9-13: "After this manner therefore pray ye: Our Father which art in heaven, Hallowed be thy name, Thy kingdom come. Thy will be done in earth, as it is in heaven. Give us this day our daily bread. And forgive us our debts, as we forgive our debtors. And lead us not into temptation, but deliver us from evil: for thine is the kingdom, and the power, and the glory, forever. Amen."

### *Model vs. Ritual*

Jesus was not giving a ritual prayer to be recited word for word. He said, "After this manner, therefore pray ye." He did not say, "Pray these exact words."

We don't find the first century church repeating this prayer in their services. We have no record in the Bible of a disciple reciting this prayer. We have some prayers recorded, and they are different. Jesus didn't command a stereotyped prayer. Rather, he encouraged natural, meaningful, from-the-heart praying. Just talking to God when praying.

We should say, however, that it's proper to use every item in this prayer today, except one. At the time this prayer was given it was proper to pray, "Thy kingdom come;" but it is not today. The kingdom has come. It came on the first Pentecost after the resurrection of Christ, as recorded in Acts 2. At the time when they were praying, "thy kingdom come," they also were preaching "the kingdom is at hand" (Matthew 4:17 and 10:7). After Pentecost the message was different. The prayers were different also. The message was that men were already being "translated into the kingdom of God's dear Son" (Colossians 1:13); and we find no one praying, "Thy kingdom come," nor being taught to do so. It is no more appropriate to pray, thy kingdom come," than it is to preach, "the kingdom is at hand."

There is no Bible reason to conclude the phrase, "The kingdom is at hand" and "Thy kingdom come" refer to two different things. These phrases were used during the same period, and they stopped being used in Scripture at the same time. At the time when people were expecting the kingdom to come soon, what was more natural than to pray, "Thy kingdom come." There's no necessity for believing that everything Jesus taught during his personal ministry, applies to us today. Jesus lived under the old covenant and taught the people to keep the law of Moses. He even commanded the offering of animal sacrifices (Matthew 8:4). This certainly does not apply today. Why then should we think that everything in the model prayer (without exception) must be applied today? The fact that according to history men soon began to use the model prayer as a ritual doesn't prove that it should be done. All we have to guide us is the Bible.

## Analysis

Observe that there are two sections to the model prayer. They are:

1. Praise and thanksgiving

2. Petitions

This constitutes the best outline for you to follow in making a prayer. *(1)* Under the heading of Praise and Thanksgiving, we first notice the statement, "Our Father." This is an expression which recognizes God's tender love and care. It shows one's confidence in, and appreciation for, the never failing love or our fatherly God.

The statement, "Which art in heaven," confesses that God is above all things, looking over us and upon us. They are words of reverence and praise to the great God of heaven. As it is said in 1 Chronicles 20:6b, "Art thou not God in heaven, and rulest thou nor over the kingdoms of the heathen?"

"Hallowed be thy name," is saying, "Holy, or set apart, is thy name." These are words of reverence and praise, which recognize God's holiness.

*(2)* Under the heading, Petitions, we find the first two requests are in behalf of the things of God ("Thy kingdom come, thy will be done in earth, as it is in heaven"). These petitions speak of one's love and concern for the kingdom of God and the will of God. They say he is interested in the

kingdom. They say he wants to see men on earth become as obedient as the angels of heaven. They express a missionary spirit. They show a zeal for evangelism.

The remaining petitions are for the fulfilling of man's needs. By employing the plural pronoun "our" and "us," the Lord indicated that you should pray for others as well as for yourself. It is, "give us our daily bread" rather then, "give me." Jesus prayed for others, and Paul exhorted that prayers "be made for all men" (John 17:9,20; 1 Timothy 2:1). So should we pray for others.

## Summary

From the model prayer you learn that it is good to start your prayers by praising the Lord and giving him thanks. "Enter into his gates with thanksgiving and into his courts with praise: be thankful unto him and bless his name" (Psalms 100:4). When you get into the petitions, it is good to first ask for God's blessings upon the things of the Lord, such as the church and the efforts to win souls. Then after this ask for things for yourself and others, things you have reason to believe are in keeping with the divine will. Material needs such as daily bread. Spiritual needs such as forgiveness of sins.

If you keep this simple outline in mind it will help you form your prayers. Not all prayers of the Bible follow this outline, and the Lord was not asking you to be a slave to it. However, many of the prayers do follow the outline.

The prayer in Acts 4:24-30 follows this general, two-part outline and shows the early disciples learned something from the model prayer given to them by the Lord.

*(1)* First is praise and thanksgiving, "Lord, thou art God, which hast made heaven, and earth and the sea, and all that in them is: who by the mouth of thy servant David hast said, Why did the heathen rage, and the people imagine vain

things? The kings of the earth stood up, and the rulers gathered together against the Lord, and against his Christ. For of a truth against thy holy child Jesus, whom thou hast anointed, both Herod, and Pontius Pilate, with the Gentiles, and the people of Israel, were gathered together for to do whatsoever thy hand and thy council determined beforehand to be done."

*(2)* The petition part contains only one request: "And now, Lord, behold their threatenings: and grant unto thy servants, that with all boldness, they may speak thy word, by stretching forth thine hand to heal; and that signs and wonders may be done by the name of thy holy child Jesus." They petitioned for boldness and effectiveness in their preaching.

For other New Testament prayers which follow this outline see Ephesians 3:14-19; Acts 1:24,25. Many Old Testament prayers follow the same sort of outline. It is an excellent way for you.

The outline:

    I. Praise and Thanksgiving

    II.Petitions

        (1) Concerning the things of the
           Lord, and

        (2) Concerning our needs

The model prayer may be analyzed in different ways. It expresses the right attitudes. It expresses reverence and praise ("Our Father which art in heaven, hallowed be thy name"). It expresses loyalty ("Thy kingdom come"). The evangelistic spirit ("Thy will be done in earth"). Dependence and reliance ("Give us ... bread ... lead us not into temptation"). Trust ("This day our daily bread"). Penitence ("Forgive us"). And the forgiving attitude ("As we forgive"). The prayer expresses the proper spirit; the spirit we should have when praying to God.

Another impression you are bound to get from reading the model prayer is that your prayers should be simple, direct and sincere.

So I conclude by saying, "After this manner therefore pray ye."

## *Other Bible Prayers*

You will profit greatly by studying the various prayers found in your Bible. Besides the ones mentioned above, it's suggested that you read and study those listed below.

2 Samuel 7: 18-29

1 Kings 8:22-61

1 Chronicles 29:10-19

Nehemiah 1:5-11

Isaiah 37:14-20

Daniel 9:4-19

Psalm 51

Matthew 26:39

John 12:27,28

John 17

One thing to notice as you read all these prayers is how the people who prayed were specific when they made their requests to God. Surely it is better that we not just make general and broad petitions. A boy wanting a new bicycle doesn't say, "Daddy, buy me something I'll enjoy." No, he asks for a bike specifically. In the same way you can name your needs. It is also well, when praying for the sick, to call out the name of each one for whom you are praying.

## Exercise

1. Taking the prayer that Jesus gave (Matthew 6 and Luke 11) as your model write out what would be proper opening words for a prayer (words of praise and thanksgiving). Use no more than 60 words at the very most. The book of Psalms furnishes many beautiful phrases of praise and thanksgiving.

2. Do this a second time, in a different way.

3. What proportion of the following prayer is made up of praise and thanksgiving: 1 Chronicles 29:10-19?

4. What proportion of the prayer in Nehemiah 1:5-11?

5. What proportion of the prayer in Isaiah 37:14-20?

# CHAPTER FOUR
## How to Pray at Home

A t home is the first place to start praying, and praying at home is the easiest way to gain experience. As soon as one becomes a Christian he should start praying privately.

Regardless of how inadequate the new Christian feels about his ability to pray, he must start. God doesn't expect one to start out as a polished prayer-maker. You learn to do by doing. You profit by your mistakes. You improve as you go along.

The instructions you have already received to this point are enough to get you started praying at home. You have learned from chapter two how to offer a prayer that will be answered. In chapter three you have studied the model prayer. Model your private prayers after this one. At least, attempt to do so. Start out with words of praise and thanksgiving, then make your petitions. It is that simple. In making petitions, plan to pray for the things of the Lord, then for things needed by you and your family and by others. Remember, however, that it isn't essential that you follow this, or any other form. The examples of Jesus and his disciple are proof enough on this point.

Don't be so afraid of making a mistake that you hesitate to start.

### *Praying With Other Family Members*

Every time the family sits down for a meal you have an opportunity to pray together. In the evenings and at other times it is important to have family prayers. A Christian family I knew in Australia, would always stop and pray together before getting into their car to make a trip. A Christian mother once told me of making it a steadfast rule to pray with her young son before he left for school each morning.

There is much truth in the saying, "The family that prays together, stays together." And what an important thing it is to keep the family together. What a difficult thing it can be, too in these times. However, keeping the family together is not the only value in praying together. We are not just interested in the by-products of praying. We believe God answers prayer. That he will help us if we ask him. He will fill our needs. We believe also that through our prayers God will be influenced to help others, as we pray for the church and the nations, for this old world and for individuals in need. There's added value in united prayer; and this is what we have when we pray at home with the members of our family.

Jesus said, "Enter into thy closet, and when thou hast shut the door, pray to thy Father which is in secret; and thy Father which seeth in secret shall reward thee openly" (Matthew 6:6).

Private praying is a test of your sincerity. Also of your faith in the Lord and in his promise to answer prayer. The hypocrite or the unbeliever may enter into prayer sessions with others, but he won't do much praying while alone.

The Lord wants us to be a praying people, and here's where to begin. Jesus prayed much when alone with the Father. In the very brief accounts we have of his life on earth, we are told a great deal about his private prayer life. "He . . . withdrew into the wilderness and prayed." "And it came to pass in those days that he went out into the mountain to pray, and continued all night in prayer to God." "And it came to pass, as he was alone praying . . . " "And when he had sent the multitude away, he went up into a mountain apart to pray . . . " "And in the morning, arising up a great deal before day, he went out, and departed into a solitary place, and there prayed." He agonized in prayer alone with God in Gethsemane. See Luke 5:16; 6:12; 9:18; Matthew 14:23; Mark 1:35 and 14:32.

There are some helpful externals to praying. Such things as the place where you pray and the posture of your body. I have already said that no certain posture is essential. This doesn't mean that posture can't be helpful. In some of his praying, Jesus knelt; he fell on the ground; he looked up to heaven. See Luke 22:41; Mark 14:35; 6:41; John 17:1. You will do well to take the time to stop and assume a reverent posture when you pray alone.

Jesus inferred the need for a place to pray, when he said, "Enter into thy closet, and when thou hast shut the door, pray to thy Father which is in secret." There are times when Jesus prayed in the hearing of other people (John 11:41,42); which proves it isn't wrong to do so. Yet he said to enter your closet and shut the door. Brother, you will find it helpful to have a place where you can get off to yourself; at least at times. Your inner closet may be a lonely trail through the woods or a solitary place beside a river. It may be your bedroom or your study or workshop. Have some place where you can steal away and stop and say your prayers.

Say your prayers. Don't just think them. In Matthew 6 there are given some words one may say in private prayer. Take the time to say the prayer. It is generally more respectful to do so. And you will find it more helpful.

Have a time to pray. Times (I should say). Definite times. Schedule them. Otherwise you may go through the day, giving the Lord only the crumbs. You may go through the day without praying at all. First, the day should be started off with prayer. It should be closed with prayer. And there should be definite times during the day for prayer.

David once said, "Evening and morning, and at noon will I pray . . . " (Psalms 55:17).

Budget the necessary time for private prayer. None of us has the time, except as he makes it. Don't try to do it in your spare time. Prayer deserves something better. And your plan won't work, if you try to pray just in your spare time. Budget some of your prime time. You will get more work done as a result. Perhaps you should get up ten minutes earlier each morning to pray. Jesus was known to have risen a great while before the day that he might go out into a desert place and pray (Mark 1:35). It is said that John Wesley's mother, having a very large family, arose early before the busy day commenced, that she might spend some time with God.

Decide on a plan. One that will work for you. The following suggestions may help: *(1)* designate a time and place, *(2)* read a short selection from the Scriptures, *(3)* having thus become more conscious of the nearness of the Lord, lift up your heart in praise and thanksgiving, and *(4)* continue to pray for others and yourself, as well as the things of the Lord.

Make a list of people and things you want to mention in prayer. Maintain an intelligent interest in the work of the church. Pray for your elders, preachers and teachers. For your fellow-members, especially the new and weak Christians. Why not remember by name those missionaries you know or know of, and ask the Lord of harvest to send forth more laborers? Pray for your unsaved friends, too. Pray for your enemies. Pray for the rulers of the nation and the world.

## WHEN I PRAY

I do not always bend the knee to pray,

I sometimes pray in crowded city streets,

In some hard crisis of a busy day
Prayer is my sure, my comforting retreat.
Dear Lord, Thy help! My lips cry silently.
From swiftly speeding car my prayer ascends;
Heaven is not far, but near to me;
And ever from his throne my Father bends.
Here at my daily task I need his aid;
No matter where I am I crave his care.
In moments when my soul is most afraid,
It comforts me to know that he is there.

-Author unknown

You may want to pause in the middle of some task to whisper, Thank you, Lord. As you enter some difficult job you may say under your breath, Lord, Please help. In the middle of the night, you may lie there in silent communion with your Lord. But you are not so likely to do these things, unless you do the other things I was talking about. Let me urge you to have a time and place for private praying. Assume a posture. Say words. Then try to stay in communion with the Lord the rest of the day.

## *Prayer Before Meals*

Perhaps I should say, Thanksgiving before meals. Thanksgiving is the first concern at meal-time. God has created meats "to be received with thanksgiving . . . Nothing is to be rejected if it be received with thanksgiving, for it is sanctified through the word of God and prayer" (1 Timothy 4:3-5). At Emmaus, our Lord, "When he sat down with them to eat, he took the bread and blessed; and breaking it he gave to them" (Luke 24:30). Following the noble example of his Lord, Paul, when he had taken bread "gave thanks in the presence of them all" (Acts 27:35).

My brother in Christ, it is imperative that you give thanks for the food you eat. It is imperative that you teach your children to be thankful for their food; to recognize that it comes from God as a gift.

If you do no more than pause before eating, and say, "Thank you, Lord, in Jesus' name," it will be acceptable. However, there's nothing wrong in extending this thanksgiving prayer before a meal. A few other things could be included. This could be one of the times when you pray with your family about some things that concern you all. You can express thanks, not only for food, but for one another and for your happy home, etc. It is well to include a short petition for the church; and it is never out of order to ask for forgiveness. However, it is probably wise to keep this prayer relatively short.

## Teach Your Children to Pray

The wise man said, "Train up a child in the way he should go" (Proverbs 22:6). The way a child should go is the way of prayer. This is a part of it, surely. So, train your child to pray.

Your example is the main thing. If he observes that you believe in praying, he is more likely to believe in it. But if you do no more than set the example, he may come to wonder why you do not take the time to talk to him about prayer and teach him to pray the same as you teach him to be courteous and to do a good job at his work and play.

Pray with your children and ask them to pray. Start by doing this at meal time and bed time. Start this when they are very young. Help them to develop a good attitude toward prayer. Lead them to think of it as a privilege more than a duty.

## PRAYER

I got up early one morning

And rushed right into the day!

I had so much to accomplish

That I didn't have time to pray.

Problems just tumbled upon me

And heavier came each task.

"Why doesn't God help me?" I wondered.

He answered, "You didn't ask."

I wanted to see joy and beauty

But the day toiled on, grey and bleak.

I wondered why God didn't show me.

He said, "But you didn't seek."

I woke up early this morning

And paused before entering the day.

I had so much to accomplish

That I had to take time to pray.

                              -Anonymous

### *Exercise*

1.   In Matthew 6:6, exactly what did Jesus mean by "thy closet"?

2.   Outline a schedule for your family (or some family) to pray together every day. Make the schedule light enough to be workable. Give times and places for the prayer sessions.

3.   Do the same for your praying alone each day.

# CHAPTER FIVE

## How to Join In, When Prayer is Led by Someone Else

**D**o you have a clear understanding of the difference between private and public prayers?

The difference is simple. We have an example in Acts 4:23-30 of a public (group) prayer. A group of disciples were together, and had a common concern. We are told, "They lifted up their voice to God with one accord." Then we are given the exact words they said in praying together. It was likely a prayer that any one of them might have said, except they prayed together. It was a united prayer. It was a "one accord" prayer. Not only did they all pray at once. They all prayed the same thing. They even used the same words. We have the wording given.

This is different from what happens in some groups today. One time in Lubbock, Texas I had occasion to go into the edifice of a certain church, looking for the minister. The doors were open, so I walked in. Going to the end of the hall, I saw through an open doorway, four men standing with heads bowed. They were praying; and I was near enough to hear them. I did not understand what was being said, however; for they were all talking at once. All were speaking aloud at the same time. No one was listening to what another was saying. No doubt, they called this praying together. But they were not all praying the same thing. Had the words been put into writing, there would have been four prayers; not one. What these four men were doing was confusing to me. Had the meeting been larger the confusion would have been worse. In a congregation of one hundred or more, such praying would have sounded as if bedlam had broken forth. And the Scriptures say, "God is not the author of confusion" (1 Corinthians 14:33).

Of the two situations, the one that was orderly was the one in the book of Acts. This was the prayer calculated to be helpful to everyone who might be in the meeting.

How can a group of people pray with "one accord" like this, all praying the same words? How can this be managed? This can be done by having one man lead. Let him word the prayer, and let the others follow with their thoughts and their amens. In Bible days, when the church would come together, people were told to pray so that others could understand. They were told, "Else when thou shalt bless with the spirit, how shall he that occupieth the room of the unlearned say Amen at thy giving of thanks, seeing he understandeth not what thou sayest?" (1 Corinthians 14:16). In other words, one man could word a prayer, and the others could say, Amen. The amens do not need to be said audibly every time. They may be, so long as confusion is not caused. To say amen in your heart is to join with what is being said. You join in a public prayer when you follow the prayer with your thoughts and say amen in your heart. This is participating in public prayer.

### Participant vs. Spectator

If you are a Christian you attend church meetings to participate in worship. The prayer leader is not a performer, with the others as the audience. All are performers, and God is the audience.

As a Christian you are a priest. You are one who offers up worship for yourself. You don't depend on another to do it for you. It shouldn't be that one brother does the praying for the church. The whole church should pray. One brother can lead. The others can enter into the prayer with him.

You attend in order to worship the Lord. You do this by eating the Lord's Supper, by singing, by praying, etc. You do these things yourself. You can't worship by proxy. You may not say a word aloud during the prayers; but you participate just the same.

## There's Added Value Here

There is added value in united prayer. Jesus once said to his apostles, "Again I say unto you, that if two of you shall agree on earth as touching anything that ye shall ask, it shall be done for them of my Father which is in heaven. For where two or three are gathered together in my name, there am I in the midst of them" (Matthew 18:19, 20). Assembling with the church and joining in the prayers means much to the child of God. And the Bible admonishes, "not forsaking the assembling of yourselves together . . . " (Hebrews 10:25). Attend. But don't just attend. Join in.

## When Not to Participate in a Prayer

There can be places and times when you should not join in the prayers. When you should be just a visitor; not a participant. You may be visiting some meeting where it would be wrong to participate. Wrong, because the things being done are unscriptural. God is not pleased, and you cannot afford to become a party to it. Notice the principle, as laid down in 2 John 9-11: "Whosoever transgresseth and abideth not in the doctrine of Christ, hath not God . . . If there come any unto you,and bring not this doctrine, receive him not into your house, neither bid him God-speed: for he that biddeth him God-speed is a partaker in his evil deeds."

You don't want to take part in things which are displeasing to God. So don't participate in the prayers when you simply cannot afford to do so. Just be an innocent by-stander. Be courteous. Listen and learn what you can. But don't participate.

## *Overcoming Distractions*

Annoying distractions will make it difficult for you to really enter into the prayer, sometimes. These may be noises or other outside distractions. The problem may be your own wandering thoughts. Whatever causes them, there are ways of overcoming distractions.

*1.* Be interested. Make sure you are. Be interested before you get to the assembly. Surely you want to pray with your brethren. Really want to. Surely there are things for which you desire to pray unitedly. It may be a special evangelistic effort about to get under way. There may be someone whom you are trying to lead to Christ. There should always be. Perhaps a brother is seriously ill and needs the prayers of the church. You are surely interested in the growth of the church, her unity and success. What a privilege it is to join with your brethren in praying about such things. And there are many other things that call for united praying. Remind yourself of this fact. It will sharpen your interest. You will look forward joyfully to the moment when prayers are called for. If you are interested, those little distractions are not likely to spoil your prayers.

*2.* Say Amen. Say it all along as the prayer progresses, under your breath. This will help to make you an active participant. It doesn't have to be the word, amen, every time. You may say, Yes, Lord. Please, Lord. Thank you, God. Or something like that.

*3.* Exercise self-discipline. Practice disciplining your thoughts. Self-control is one of the seven Christian virtues to be added with all diligence (2 Peter 1:5-11). You can't expect the surroundings to be ideal always. It is up to you to learn some self-discipline.

An effort should be made by our leaders to have quietness in worship. To avoid distractions. But this cannot always be done. I am persuaded the emphasis doesn't belong on trying to create an ideal atmosphere. The main responsibility is on each individual worshipper. Little distractions don't need to spoil one's worship. Think of the situation at the foot of the cross when our Lord was put to death. We talk about and sing about coming to the foot of the cross. Have you considered the noise and confusion that must have been there? The Roman soldiers surely did not make a studied effort to be quiet. The bystanders shouted insults at the Christ. Yet, neither Mary nor John nor any other disciple who was there would have had trouble in centering his thoughts on Christ. Today, we can usually rise above the situation, whatever it is, and manage to enter into the worship.

If we fail to emphasize self-discipline and seek to solve the problem solely by creating an atmosphere of quietness, we may pay a dear price for it. We may even create a congregation of snobs. People who neglect to be friendly with one another and with the visitors. There is no substitute for self-discipline.

4. Often times you are able to remove yourself from the distracting situation. You can change pews. You can sit closer to the front. You can remove yourself from the whisperers and those who play with babies during the service.

5. You will find it helpful to come early and sit quietly a few minutes before the program is to commence. This will give you a little time to prime your heart; to generate a spirit of worship.

6. Participate, not only in the prayers, but in all acts of worship. As a result you will pray better.

*7.* Pray privately. Pray at home, and it will be more natural for you to enter into the public prayers. Pray privately before you leave home. Ask the Lord to help you worship acceptably that day. Surely God will delight in answering such a prayer.

*8.* Make up your mind that you will not be frustrated if the prayer leader fails to do as good a job as he should. He may leave unsaid a number of things you are interested in praying about. Perhaps in the next prayer these things will be mentioned. If not, at least you can add them to your own prayer under your breath. Likely the prayer leader will do an acceptable job most of the time. Perhaps you can encourage the brethren to improve in the leading of prayers. Suggest a training class. Or that individuals purchase this or some other book on how to pray. Present a book as a gift to one or more of them.

*9.* Practice makes perfect. The more often you attend the meetings and participate, the more satisfaction you will derive from the prayers. You learn to do by doing. That's how you learn to overcome distractions. That's how you learn to participate in the public prayers in a satisfying way.

*10.* Discuss the problem with others. Learn how other people overcome distractions. Ask them, "Tell me, what is the best way you have found to avoid distractions and enter into the spirit of worship?" You are likely to get some fresh and helpful ideas.

## *Conclusion*

Things are inter-related. You are not likely to pray well unless you do at least a fair job in the other areas of Christian endeavor. You will grow in the area of prayer during the time you are experiencing Christian growth generally. You will not succeed as a praying person unless you succeed as a Christian. This being true, I want to close this chapter by giving a workable formula for successful Christian living. There are five things for you to give careful attention to. There are other things about Christian living; but if you take care of these, I don't think it likely that you will neglect the others. These five things are things that everyone can do. So, attend to these and see how the other matters seem to take care of themselves.

*(1)* Pray every day. *(2)* Study your Bible daily. *(3)* Attend all service of the congregation that it is possible for you to attend. *(4)* Take an active part. *(5)* Strive to win souls. Whether or not you succeed, try to win souls.

This formula will work for you. Give it a fair try. You will pray better. You will be a better Christian.

## *Exercise*

1.   In your own words, write down the difference between a private and a public prayer.

2.   Are you satisfied with the quality of your participation in worship? Yes___. No____.

3.   Using the book to help you, summarize the 10 ways of overcoming distractions during public worship.

4.   Underscore the ones you have never tried seriously.

5.   List on paper (or be prepared to discuss in class) the main things you do to overcome these distractions.

# CHAPTER SIX
## How To Lead In Prayer

It is most likely that fear is your greatest drawback, if you are a beginner. Don't be afraid. Leading in prayer is not difficult. You can do it if you are one who prays privately and surely you are if you are a Christian.

Do you offer thanks before meals at home? Good. You are already leading in prayer three times a day.

You need not be afraid to undertake your first public prayer today. Or next Sunday. Consider the things you already know about prayer. Think about the situation. Study this chapter. Then get started with your prayer leading. Don't stop with this, however. You will need to improve. You will need to keep studying your Bible and the prayers found in it. You will need to come back to this chapter many times. Also to the other parts of this book. You will need to gain experience. To learn from every possible source.

We are now ready to discuss how you can lead in prayer.

### Think Of Yourself As Spokesman
### For The Group

Understand and keep in mind the difference between a private and public prayer. We have already seen what the disciples did when they prayed together. "They lifted up their voice to God with one accord" (Acts 4:24). Evidently one man spoke the prayer aloud, and the others joined him in their thoughts and with their amens. The leader had an understanding of the group. He also understood the occasion that brought them together. Thus, he could express a prayer suitable to them all. It is very likely that you understand the congregation and its thinking well enough to express a prayer for the whole group. Certainly this is true if you have been a member of the church for any length of time and have taken an interest in the work and in Bible study. Surely you could word a prayer to which others could say, "Amen."

Once the mayor of a certain town had a visit from a delegation of nine citizens. There was a project they were interested in seeing him support. Before they reached his office, they designated one of their group as spokesman. When they entered the mayor's office this man did the talking. But as the mayor listened and looked into the faces of the delegation, he knew that the appeal was not coming from just one man. He could tell from the expressions on the faces of the others that they were entering into the appeal. All were speaking to him through the one. A public prayer is like this. The man designated to lead in prayer is the spokesman chosen by the group. He does all the talking; but God can see that the others are entering into the prayer. He knows this is not just the prayer of one person, but of the congregation. It is a united prayer.

So think of yourself as the spokesman for the group.

### Pray A Prayer That Fits

A few years ago, so I'm told, when J. E. Mullins, a well-known gospel preacher, was conducting a funeral, he called on a brother in the congregation to lead a prayer. It seems this brother had only one prayer. He said the very same words in all the prayers he led, and this was to be no exception. He started out by saying, "Father we thank thee for the happy occasion that brings us together."

This true story illustrates the need for fitting the prayer to the people and the occasion. You know enough about the people and the occasion to qualify as spokesman. You are to speak, not for yourself alone, but for them all. Make sure that what you say can be amened by all. You know whether or not it is something that all should be able to endorse, and something that should fit the needs of the hour. Naturally you will learn to fit the needs better as you learn more about praying and get more experience. Right now, you can do it after a fashion, at least. You can lead in prayer now.

If it is in a hospital room where you are called on to lead, your prayer will naturally be different from one you would say at the communion table on Sunday. You realize that even though you pray nicely about many things, if you do not pray for the person on the sick bed, you do not pray well. Your prayer does not fit the occasion. On the other hand, it would not be very appropriate to pray for the sick when you are offering thanks at the communion table.

If you are the prayer leader, you are not there to say your private prayers. They can be said at home. Pray for things that fit the group and the occasion. A few years ago I spent the night in the home of Frank and Billie Burger in Fort Worth, Texas. Frank and I were the last to go to bed, and before retiring we each said a prayer. Partially, they were our private prayers. I remember that Frank called the names of his children and grandchildren and asked for something specific for each one. That was good. It would not be good, however, in a prayer at the assembly of the church; and Frank does not pray like that publicly. If he did, fairness would require that he gather information enough to also mention a specific need that each one has. This would be unreasonable; thus not fitting.

You can know that two things are always fitting in a prayer: *(1)* to offer praise and thanksgiving to the Lord, and *(2)* to ask for forgiveness. The prayer of Acts 4 began with praises being offered to the Lord. This prayer is made up mostly of praises. The model prayer given by Jesus in

Matthew 6 opens with words of praise. This prayer also includes a request for forgiveness. The Lord always deserves praise and thanksgiving, and we are always making mistakes which need to be forgiven. While some Bible prayers do not include these things, they are never out of place. Besides these two things, a prayer should include that which the occasion requires. For example, if you are wording the prayer at the beginning of a Bible class, it is good to *(1)* offer praises and thanksgivings, *(2)* ask for forgiveness, *(3)* pray God's blessings on the teacher, and *(4)* on the students. This is a good prayer for the occasion. Other things could be included, but they are not so important for this prayer.

### *Make It Short Enough*

How long should your prayer be? This is a matter of judgement. You should use good judgment, however. It is usually wise to keep the prayer short. Collin Smith of Australia told of a time in Tasmania when a brother led in prayer for fifty-five minutes by the watch. Some young person timed him. Now, we can't say a prayer is sinful because it is long. Jesus prayed some long prayers. But on the occasion in Tasmania, I wonder how well the people were able to follow a fifty-five minute prayer. Evidently some of the youth had difficulty in trying it. Likely the older people did too. No doubt there were other things on the program that day besides the prayer. I would say the leader must have passed up some good opportunities to say, Amen.

Prayers don't have to be long; and can be very short. In Luke 18:13 there is found a prayer of seven words. In Matthew 14:30 there is one of three words. Both prayers were answered. One prayer was, "God, be merciful to me a sinner." The other, "Lord save me." So, don't be afraid to say a short prayer, whether or not you are a beginner.

People usually learn to pray by listening to others. This is very helpful, too. Sometimes, however, we can get wrong ideas this way. Some think they should pray the "standard" length of time; especially if it is an opening prayer they are leading. People sometimes say, "If I cannot think of enough to say to take up the standard length of time, I will mess things up." But ask yourself, who standardized the length of a prayer? The Lord certainly did not. So forget about standard lengths.

Not everything has to be included in a prayer. Christians should pray about everything, but not necessarily in one prayer. In the prayer of Acts 4 there is only one petition. Why should it not be right to have only one petition in an opening prayer? Once in a while, it might be a really good thing. There's something to be said for variety.

Remember there will be other prayers in the service. Also, Christians pray privately.

Don't misunderstand me. It is nearly always, if not always, good to include several things. Especially in the opening or main prayer. If there are sick people in the congregation, their names should be brought before the throne of God. If they are not included in this prayer, there ought to be a special prayer in their behalf. The same is true in behalf of those who have lost loved ones recently. The same applies if there's a brother ready to depart your community for the mission fields. There are other situations where this would apply. Brethren ought to pray for one another. Ought to pray together for one another. This is brotherhood. This is love.

The preacher needs the prayer of the congregation. So do the elders and deacons. And the new members. God's blessings should be called down upon the program of the church and on special programs that are in the planning. Missionaries should not be forgotten when we pray. We are told to pray for world leaders. At times there are special problems in our country or among the other nations, such as the threat of war. We should find some place to pray about such things. The poor, the hungry, the captive should not be forgotten. Many things cry out for an interest in our prayers. It is obvious that we cannot mention them all in every prayer. Some things, more than others, should be included. When one is first beginning to lead in prayer, he should not even try to include everything which he feels would be good. He should keep his prayer short. Later he will get to the place where more of these things will be included. Even so, there is a limit. Don't think that the more a prayer includes, the better it is. Sometimes it is the other way around.

In the heading of this section, you notice I did not say, make your prayer long enough. That's not the common problem. Making it short enough is. It should be short enough that vain repetitions will not likely creep in. Short enough that the minds of the people will not wander.

## *Make Yourself Both Heard And Understood*

During the formative days of the church, when some people had miraculous spiritual gifts, such as tongues-speaking, Paul said they should not pray in an unknown tongue in the assembly. He said, "Else when thou shalt bless with the spirit, how shall he that occupieth the room of the unlearned say Amen at thy giving of thanks, seeing he understandeth not what thou sayest?" (1 Corinthians 14:16). The people have to understand "what thou sayest" if they are to say Amen, and thus enter into the prayer.

If you speak too softly, for example, the people cannot follow the prayer. In every congregation there are those whose voices are soft. That's why a public address system usually is provided. By going to the microphone, one can make himself heard easily, even if there are noises. Use the microphone. Encourage others to do the same. At least, do something so it will be certain that all will hear you. Stand and face the audience, at least. Suppose the song leader should lead from one of the back pews, without even standing and should sing in a very small voice. Those at a distance from him wouldn't know when to start singing. They couldn't tell which verse to sing. Suppose the preacher should move away from the mike, turn his back to the congregation and speak in a very low voice. How long would he be in demand? Yes, do something so as to be heard when you lead in prayer.

Also make sure you are understood. Not only use simple language, but speak slowly and distinctly.

You must be heard and understood.

## *Pray Simply*

Simplicity is primary. You have been hearing the older brethren pray beautiful prayers. They often use striking and poetic phrases. You may be inclined to think you must do the same. Not so. I am not saying it is wrong to do some of this, as you gain experience. Many of the Psalms are prayers, and they are poems. There are many beautiful expressions in them. Such is surely not wrong. Sometimes it is helpful, as it stirs the emotions and helps people get into a better frame of mind for worship. But, if you are just starting out, leave this to the future. Jesus gave a simple little prayer as a model . We find other prayers in the Bible that are very simple. It is a bit dangerous to try for the artistic in praying. It can lead to superficiality. At least, it can sound superficial, and that will distract the worshippers. Studiously avoid hypocrisy. Avoid praying to be heard of men. To impress people rather than God. Take heed that you do not your righteousness before men to be heard of them. See Matthew 6:1, RV.

As time goes on, and you grow in ability, give some thought to poetic language; but be careful with it. Some people are not poetic, and should not try to be. It doesn't matter. Simplicity and sincerity are first rate. Today, even many of the arts are swinging to the simple. This is true of the speech arts. In years gone by the student of public speaking was taught oratory. He gave declamations in high sounding tones. But today, he is told that the best style is conversational. And this is catalogued as, The Speech Arts. In the art of writing the same is true. "Write as you would talk," they say. In view of this, don't under rate simplicity in prayer.

The late W. W. Otey, gospel preacher, once told of his first attempt at leading in prayer. He had been baptized recently near his home in the mountains in Virginia. A service was being conducted, and the preacher, J. T. Showalter, asked Otey to lead in prayer. He undertook it, but stalled out in mid-air. Brother Showalter had to finish the prayer for him. He said, "I later asked him, 'Brother Showalter, tell me how to overcome embarrassment in praying in public.' His answer was brief. 'Think more about the Lord and less about what the hearers are thinking.'" Brother, that's good advice.

## Get Started: Keep Going: Keep Growing

You learn to do by doing. Forget your fears and get started. Let the elders of the congregation know you are ready to try leading in prayer. You might feel better starting with a dismissal prayer or a prayer at the communion table.

And what if you make mistakes. Everyone had to face this problem in the beginning. Had all the other people given in to this fear, there would be no one today to lead in prayer. When you say the wrong thing, just start the sentence over and say it right. No one expects you to be perfect. Someone has said, "The way to succeed is to make mistakes, and more mistakes, and still more mistakes; and to make fewer and fewer mistakes all the time."

Get started and keep going. Take advantage of every opportunity to lead in prayer; and strive to do a better job every time.

To help you get started, I suggest you take these steps:

a.   Decide which prayer (for example, the dismissal).

b.   Ask yourself, What are the things that must be included in this kind of prayer?

c.   Ask, What is there about the occasion that should be considered?

d.   Decide what you want to say in your opening statements of praise and thanksgiving; commit to memory both the opening and closing statements. These should be short, possibly one sentence, or at the most two. Include, "in the name of Christ" in your closing statement.

e.   Determine if you will include a request for forgiveness.

f.   What requests do you want to make in behalf of the Lord's things (the church, a missionary, a special program of work, etc.).

g. What requests do you want to make for yourself and the others (improvement in health, help in living right, God's presence as we go out, journeying mercies, or whatever). Do not work out the exact wording. You want to be able to remember the subjects and speak of them in a natural way as the words come to you.

h.   Get off to yourself and practice prayer; but don't plan on giving it exactly as you have practiced it. It may help to write it out; but be sure to destroy the writing before you give the prayer.

i.   Remind yourself that if you forget something, it will not be disastrous.

j.    Now, go to the brother in charge and tell him you are ready to be called on for the prayer. If he fails to use you immediately, be patient. If he seems to forget you, just go to him again.

When you have led your first prayer, then keep going and growing. Maybe you started months, or even years ago. Keep going and growing. As in other things you need to grow as a prayer leader. Don't become satisfied with yourself because you are able to lead in prayer anytime you are called upon. Study. Expand your mind. Try to make your prayers fresh. Make them effective, so that the congregation will find it easier to get into the spirit of the prayers. So that their prayers, as led by you, will mean more to them.

When I was a boy in a country congregation, it bothered me that the men who led in prayer just said the same things using the same words week after week. All the prayers seemed stilted. When a brother started praying, I knew what phrase would come next. I knew what he was going to say, word for word. This bothered me. Now I can see that I should have been more tolerant and understanding, but I wondered about the prayer leader's sincerity in praying the same words over and over time after time. Yet I'm sure he was sincere. I was young and intolerant. Now I am no longer young, but am still a little intolerant of this kind of praying. And there are others who are younger and more intolerant. I have people tell me this kind of praying bothers them greatly. The prayer leader doesn't realize it. He has just gotten into the habit of praying this way and has not realized the importance of improving in his prayer leading. Actually, it is not easy to change the wording from prayer to prayer. The most of us are guilty of using the same old phrases again and again. It is something we need to work on.

Grow. Try to be fresh. Study the prayers found in the Bible. Decide it is worth the effort, and you will soon see results. After you have said a prayer, go home and take up this book again. Review portions of it to see how you might have done a better job in leading the prayer. Keep growing.

## *Exercise*

1.   How many words are in the model prayer of Matthew 6? In the Lord's prayer of John 17? At the rate of 120 words per minute, how long would it take to say these prayers?

2.   Write down a verse of Scripture which teaches that public prayers need to be loud enough and distinct enough for the whole congregation to hear and understand them.

3.   What kind of compliment would you appreciate most after having led in prayer?

# CHAPTER SEVEN

## How to Work Out the Wording
## for Various Prayers

### SECTION 1

Y ou are now ready to work out the wording for your prayers. Let's say you are to lead a prayer at a given time in the future. What are you going to say? What words will you use? How will you start? How will you end the prayer?

Let me help you. When Jesus helped his disciples to pray, he gave them a model prayer. They were not asked to say it exactly as given. Nor do we find where they ever did this. They could have done so at one time or another. You could do the same today, except for the phrase, "Thy kingdom come" (for the kingdom has already come, as we saw in Chapter Three). You could make an appropriate change here and say this prayer on many occasions. It would be proper; but not necessarily the best thing for you to do. The Lord's prayer is a sample prayer. It was not meant to be used as a stereotype.

In this chapter you will be given other sample prayers. Prayers which are not found in Scripture, but are nevertheless scriptural. You can use them, or parts of them. You can borrow phrases from them if you choose. Primarily the purpose in giving them here is to stimulate your thinking and give you ideas.

## *In General*

First I just want to talk to you about the wording of a prayer and how you can work it out. It is not recommended that you read your prayers or say them from memory. If you can do so while praying naturally and sincerely, there's nothing sinful about doing it. We read prayers when we sing from our hymnals, for many of the hymns are prayers. Sometimes we sing them from memory. Surely it would not be sinful for you to do the same thing when it comes to leading in prayer. This is not wrong within itself. But—and here is the rub—it is more difficult to be natural and sincere in praying if you do this. It may also be a distraction to brethren who know you are reading the prayer, or saying it by memory. They may be tempted to think you are saying a prayer by rote. The best advice is, Don't read your prayers, Don't say them by memory. You don't need to. Not even as a beginner.

What about using notes, such as an outline? I would say that they should only be used if necessary. Then only as long as necessary while you are gaining confidence to pray without them. From the very first you can pray without using notes. You need not form a habit which will need to be broken later. It is better to go without notes. There may be two exceptions: *(1)* If you want to call the names of certain people as you pray in their behalf—a good practice—then you could have their names jotted down and in front of you while you pray; and *(2)* you might learn by memory the opening sentence and the closing sentence for the purpose of giving you confidence.

The best way to lead in prayer is to figure out ahead of time what you are going to say; but not word-for-word. Only work out the general arrangement of your prayer and the different subjects you wish to pray about. Then express yourself naturally. Just talk to God. The words will come.

They don't need to be in the form of poetry. They don't need to be beautiful words. Just make direct statements. Recall a subject you have planned to pray about and simply ad lib. You will make it through; and you will get better at this as you gain more experience.

Whether you use the pronouns of Old English or Modern English, is your choice to make. You may address God as Thee, Thou and Thine; or you may simply say You, Yours. The original language did not have special pronouns for addressing Deity. When Old English was in use, there were no special pronouns for Deity. The King James Bible, dating from 1611, uses Thee, Thou and Thine. Some later revisions have retained this form for addressing Deity. Others have not. It is not a matter of "thus said the Lord" either way. Surely God can be addressed reverently either way; and this is the important thing. Which ever way you choose to go, try to be consistent. It's not consistent to address God as Thou at one time and as You at another in the same prayer.

Surely such words as Dad and Daddy in addressing God are not considered respectful. Neither does it sound reverent to speak of God as "the old man upstairs." Even if one thinks these words and phrases can be used in complete reverence, he will surely admit they will not be so considered by all who might be praying with him. Instead of helping them to pray, he will be hindering them by using such language. That's enough to make it wrong.

### Grace at Meal-Time

When you have grace before meals, it is well to include a few items besides thanking God for your food. This is good because most of us do not pray often enough; and these can serve as three short prayers a day in which we mention some of the things that need to be prayed about. After speaking a word of praise to the Lord, it seems natural to say "thank you," not only for the food, but for such things as shelter, protection, the family , and above all for Jesus the gift of God's love. It also seems natural when one gives thanks for his blessings, to offer a prayer for those less fortunate, for the poor, the sick, the bereaved, etc. To ask for forgiveness is always in order; and it takes such little time to ask God's blessings on the church (something that should be on our minds and in our hearts at all times). There are often special problems or needs of the hour. They should be mentioned specifically. Perhaps the local church is in the midst of a special effort to win souls, or you are engaged in trying to win a certain person to Christ. You will find you can include different things in this prayer of thanksgiving, and do it briefly enough that you won't need to say, "Thank you for this *cold* food."

## *Praying Alone*

The time you will pray for many things is when you enter your "closet" to pray alone. These prayers will be more lengthy.

If you read a short scripture before you start, you will feel close to the Lord. Then begin your prayer with words of praise to God.

Thanksgiving goes with praise. This is an ideal place to thank the Lord for his blessings. Name specific blessings. It would be all right to have a list of them before you as you pray. Such things as God's love, the gift of his beloved Son, the church, the Bible, life itself, food and shelter and the comforts of life, health, loved ones, friends, sunshine and rain, freedom, your job, God's answer to your former prayers, etc., etc. Probably all of us should spend more time offering thanks for our blessings than we do in asking for things.

Having expressed your praise and thanksgiving, begin your petitions by asking God's blessings upon His things. Such as the church, specific projects in the church, the missionaries, etc.

It would be well to follow this with intercessions for other people. Such people as your elders, your preacher, various members of the congregation, especially those who are new or weak Christians, and for those who have fallen away. Call them by name. Pray for all you know who are sick or who are in distress. Those who have troubles. For all men. "Especially for them of the household of faith." For the political leaders. Pray in behalf of those who have requested your prayers.

Pray for your loved ones, naming them one-by-one. Pray for your enemies, even as the Lord teaches in Matthew 5:44.

Make specific requests for yourself and your family. The things you are working to attain. The things you earnestly want. If they are things you feel hesitant about praying for, then you should not desire them and work for them. Ask the Lord to help you in turning your interest away from them. Ask God to help you be a better Christian, to grow spiritually, to become more effective in his service and especially as a soul-winner. Request the Lord's help in overcoming your besetting sins. And, of course, ask for forgiveness.

These are some of the things you will want to pray about. Just do it in a natural, but respectful way. Use words that are natural for you. It would be foolish to try to impress the Lord with your ability to speak in eloquent language. If you make a mistake, simply stop and begin the sentence anew. Simply talk to the Lord. Know what you want to talk to him about, and talk in a simple way. Be direct. Your statements on each subject can be brief. There's no need to explain the details to the Lord for He already knows.

Perhaps you should make a list of the things about which you want to pray and the people for whom you wish to pray. Then take the list with you into your inner closet.

## *Family Prayers*

In praying with your children, give thought to their needs and pray about them. Don't make these prayers too long; and be careful to express your prayers in language that's on their level, especially if they are smaller children. Word a prayer that they can easily enter into, and that they will feel good about praying. You will want to ask your children to word some of the prayers also.

When you and your companion pray together (just the two of you), pray as two who are one flesh. Be natural. It is difficult for some people to be natural in this kind of prayer. Work on it. You will probably not try to cover all subjects in this kind of prayer. This should not take the place of your personal prayers. Every Christian needs to get off to himself and talk with God.

## *Exercise*

1. Thought question: If there are seven prayers said at home, on the same day, in how many of these prayers should one ask forgiveness?

2. Thought question: Name the item most likely to be left off the prayer list of the average Christian, in your opinion.

3. Thought question: Name three common weaknesses that many of us have regarding praying at home.

4. Examine the following private prayers: Genesis 32:9-12; Joshua 7:7-9; Judges 13:8; 2 Samuel 7:18-29; 1 Kings 3:5-9; 2 Kings 19:15-19; Jonah 2:1-9; Habakkuk 3:1-19.

5.   Read these references to private praying: 1 Samuel 1:10-17; Daniel 6:10; Matthew 6:5-7; Matthew 14:23; Acts 10:9; 1 Thessalonians 5:17.

## *Sample  Prayers*

### *Grace at Mealtime*

Our Heavenly Father: we praise your name, and offer you our sincere thanks for food and shelter, and every provision of life. You have been so very good to us. Help us to be more and more thankful for your blessings.

We pray for those who are less fortunate than we. For the poor, the sick, the troubled and those with great burdens. Bless the church, Father, and bless our work in the church.

At this time we ask your special blessings on Aunt Mary in the hospital. Be with her and with those who are seeing after her. If it be your will, restore her to good health. Bless all the sick everywhere, and especially those of your family.

In Jesus' name. Amen.

"Our Father in Heaven, we offer our thanks now for the food before us. We thank you also for our family unit. Help strengthen each of us, Dear Lord, both physically and spiritually."

In Jesus' name. Amen.

—John Coe

Dear God, our Father: We praise thee and give thee thanks for the food before us. We recognize that every good gift is from thee, and we are totally dependent on thee. Help us to be thankful always. Forgive us for the times we have been ungrateful. Forgive all our sins, we beg thee.

Father, we are thankful for the good fellowship we are enjoying together as friends and brothers, as we are together in this home. We ask thy special blessings on this home. On the father and mother. On these precious children. Also on the son who is away. Bless all our homes. Protect our families; and may we all be faithful servants of thine.

We ask thy blessings on all the poor, Father. On the sick and troubled. Upon all suffering humanity, and especially on your people.

We are thankful for the church and pray that it shall have thy blessings always.

Most of all, Father, we thank thee for Jesus, in whose name we pray. Amen.

(Note: The prayer did not include something like this, "We thank thee for these wonderful people who have invited us into their home and set this good meal before us. They are such wonderful people." You see, the prayer was said for them, as well as for the guests and the one who was leading it. For them to say Amen to a prayer which contained these last statements, would be for them to pray much like the pharisee by thanking God for what wonderful people they themselves are.

*Praying Alone*

Our Father in Heaven: Hallowed be your name. May thy church grow and have your blessings. May more and more people come to do your will, even as the angels obey you.

Give us our daily necessities; and forgive our sins, as we forgive people who do us wrong. Help us to overcome temptation.

In the name of Jesus. Amen.

Kind and loving Father; God of heaven and earth; my maker and the sustainer of my life; my Savior and my judge: hallowed be thy name.

Thank you so much Father, that I am able to approach you through Christ, My Savior, and can talk with you as friend to friend.

First, I beg you to forgive me of my sins and set me before you justified, because of Jesus and his shed blood. Please let my prayers be heard this morning.

I pray your blessings on your church; that it may grow and spread throughout the earth. I am concerned, Father, about the tendency in many places to drift away from your word. Also about the worldliness and materialism that is invading the church. Help us all with these problems. Help your church to grow. Bless those who are working to that end. Especially I ask that you bless those who have gone out to far away places to do your work, where the cause is so weak and the workers are few. O, Lord, please be with Joe and Sheryl who have gone to Old Mexico to evangelize. May they not grow weary. May they soon see fruits from their labors. Help us not to forget them. Bless the brethren at home who are supporting them. May they not grow weary in well-doing.

Please be with us at home, Father. Bless the local church. Be with our elders and the preacher; with every member. Thank you for the work that is being done. May we have greater vision and do more and more.

I pray for those who are out of Christ; that you will use me and others to reach them with the gospel. Bless those lost people who are attending the services and those involved in home studies. Please, Father, help Harry and Louise who are studying with Fran and me. Enable us to say and do the right things, so as to win them to Christ. And bless their precious children. Thank you, for giving us the opportunity to teach them.

Father, I am so grateful for Jesus and his love. That I have him as Savior and high priest through whom I can approach you. He is so wonderful to love me and die for me. Also for my wife and children, and the others of my family. Please enable me to love him more and to serve him better.

Thank you too, for my dear family. For giving me Fran as my loving companion. Bless her. Help me to make her happy. Please give us many years together in your service.

And thank you, Father for little Susie and Michael. Enable Fran and me to be good parents and to bring them up in your teaching and discipline. If it is your will, may Mike make a gospel preacher, and a good one. May Sue find her place in your vineyard, so as to do the most good with her life. Help these kids to be free of drugs and liquor and illicit sex. May they not grow up to be worldly and materialistic.

I also pray for other parents and their problems. I'm thinking especially of Henry and Helen, with the problems they are having at home. They need your help, O God. Please be with them.

There's much suffering in this world, and all around us. I beg for your help for all these people. I want to thank you, and thank you again that Aunt Mary is now out of the hospital and doing nicely. Thank you for hearing our prayers.

I'm thinking of Charles today who has had this heart operation, and of his invalid wife. These people need you more than ever now. Be near and dear to them. And use Fran and me to lift some of their burdens.

Let me say thank you for my job, for the comfortable home that we have. For so many good things. Be with us in our efforts to use all these things to glorify you.

In the name that's above every name, the name of Jesus Christ. Amen.


### *Family Prayers*

The last two example could be modified a little and used as models for family prayers.

It is hoped that these and other prayers you may read or hear will give you ideas for working out the wording for your prayers at home.


### *Personal Prayers of Jesus*

Praise for revelation to babes: Matthew 11:25,26.

Prayer for deliverance: Matthew 26:39,42,44; 27:46.

For forgiveness of others: Luke 23:34.

In submission: Luke 23:46.

At Lazarus' tomb: John 1:41,42.

For the Father's glory: John 12:27,28.

For the Church: John 17:1-26.

# CHAPTER SEVEN
## How to Work Out the Wording for Various Prayers

### SECTION 2

### *The Main Prayer in the Assembly of the Church*

By main prayer I mean the first and/or longest prayer of the service. "Main" is used to contrast this with the thanksgiving prayers at the Lord's Table, or before the collection, and with dismissals and special prayers. This is a general prayer.

Stop and think about this prayer and what it should be. *(1)* It is public prayer, led by one man in behalf of all the Christians assembled there. So it should contain the things to which all can say Amen, and things that will be satisfying to all. *(2)* It may be the only general prayer during this service; so it should include enough to be satisfactory for the general praying together of the brethren. Normally, this is not a really short prayer; but there's nothing to say it couldn't be. *(3)* If you can think of something that most of the brethren would appreciate praying together about, then include that item. For example, the church might be in the process of selecting elders, or it might be that a drought-breaking rain has come to make everyone thankful. *(4)* Ideally, it should be neither so long as to be wearisome to some of the brethren, nor so short as to fail to satisfy the main desires of the participants. *(5)* Consider that simplicity and sincerity of expression are more helpful to the participants than are beautiful and poetic phrases. Avoid "high sounding" words and words that are unnatural for you, the prayer leader.

There's no better way to build a prayer than the way the model prayer was formed. Have two main divisions to the prayer, *(1)* Praise and thanksgiving and *(2)* Petitions. Start out with some appropriate words of praise and thanksgiving. In the petition part, ask first for blessings upon the things of God, such as the kingdom and the work of evangelism.

You could start off the prayer with words like these: "Our Father in heaven, hallowed be thy name. We thank thee, Father, for our many blessings. For life itself. For food and shelter, and every material blessing. Most of all, we thank thee, Father, for thy love, for Jesus, our Saviour, and for fellowship of the Holy Spirit."

Or you could start by saying, "Heavenly Father, we bow before thee, the only true and living God. We thank thee and praise thee for all thou hast done for us. We thank thee for Jesus, thy Son and our Savior. For the Bible. For the blood-bought church. We are thankful for all our material blessings, too."

Those are simply two possible ways to start off. It is hoped that instead of using them exactly as presented, you will get ideas from them for forming a prayer that seems good and natural to you.

Here are a group of phrases, one or two of which could be used to advantage in the opening of a prayer.

Thou art a God who answers prayer; a rock in the desert where we can find shelter from the storm of life. The heavens declare thy glory, and the firmament shows thy handiwork. Thou art our shield and defender, the Ancient of days, our maker, redeemer and friend. Thou,

Lord, changeth not. From everlasting to everlasting, thou art God.

Thou art the God of the living; how excellent is thy name! Thou hast forgiven all our iniquities and redeemed us from destruction. Thou hast crowned us with lovingkindness and tender mercies. Thy mercy, O Lord, is from everlasting to everlasting upon them that fear thee. For thou, Lord, art good, and ready to forgive, and plenteous in mercy unto all them that call upon thee.

Some of the above phrases are expressions found in the Psalms. Others come from popular hymns.

A few beautiful words of praise can help make the prayer more meaningful by helping establish a better mood for worship. They were used in many of the Bible prayers. It is something to strive for, as long as the beautiful words are used naturally. The beginner, however, would be well advised not to concern himself with this. Let him not think that beauty of expression is an essential. There will be time enough for him to cultivate this after he gets the basics well in hand. If his language never acquires the poetic, he should not worry. There can be other things to make up for it, such as simplicity and sincerity. There seems to be less of the poetic in the prayers we have from Jesus, as compared to Old Testament prayers. The model prayer has a different kind of beauty. One that comes from simplicity and direct statements, chiefly.

After you have praised and thanked the Lord, sincerely and naturally, then make your petitions to him. Ask Heaven's blessings upon the things of the Lord: then pray in behalf of men's things, things that pertain to you and others.

Think ahead of time about the things you want to include in this part of the prayer. You want to pray for the local church, including the service you are in; the other services of the day; the entire program of the church. Also the church at other places, especially where it is small. Then decide on petitions to be made in behalf of yourself and the others. Such things as: "Forgive us," "Strengthen us," "Bless our sick," "Help the President and rulers of other lands," "Give us peace," etc., etc. If you end up with a great number of petitions, consider eliminating some of them. And if, when you get up to pray, you forget some of the things you intended to pray about, don't let it worry you. The brethren are free to pray privately about other things, and surely they do. That's one reason why your prayer doesn't need to be very long.

There are at least two petitions I think should always be in the "main" prayer, *(1)* a request for forgiveness and *(2)* a petition for God's blessings on the service of the hour. One could stop with these requests. However, it is well to pray for other things. The preacher who is soon to stand before the congregation would appreciate being prayed for. So would the song leader and the elders; the sick, the bereaved, the poor and the troubled. It is well to pray together about our homes. There are other things; some of which were named in the paragraph above.

May I insist that you refrain from praising the speaker of the hour or from thanking God for the man's qualities. Why? Because he is praying too. You are leading his prayer. And it ill behoves him to brag on himself in prayer to God. That's what the Pharisee did in Luke 18:9-14. You have heard prayer leaders say something like this, "Lord, we thank you for our evangelist and for his great ability; for the many sacrifices he has made." How can the faithful evangelist say Amen to a prayer like that? He would be saying, "So be it Lord, I am indeed a great man." Why not just ask the Lord to bless the preacher, to help him and use him? He, too, can say Amen to that. The other things about him can be said in your private prayers.

About the closing statements in your prayer: One sentence is enough. You could ask that the Lord be with you all; and if you have not already stated that the prayer is being made in the name of Christ, then the statement should be made here. In fact it is well to form the habit of ending all your prayers with a statement to this effect, "In the name of Christ, Amen."

It has already been said that you might want to memorize your opening sentence and your closing sentences; especially if you are a beginning prayer leader. This will mitigate the stage fright.

Make sure you don't lose volume when you come to the closing words. Otherwise the people with bowed heads won't know the prayer is finished. Give a strong amen.

### *The Main Prayer In A Bible Class*
### *Or Group Meeting*

This prayer should be much like the "main" prayer at the church assembly. Perhaps a little shorter. You can leave some things to be said at the assembly if that hour is to follow. You would *(1)* offer a few words of praise and thanksgiving, then *(2)* make some petitions that would be appropriate. Two things you would want to include are petitions for forgiveness and for God's blessings on the program of the hour. Other things too, I am sure. Ask yourself what would be appropriate, and what things are likely on the minds of the people whose prayer you will be leading. Try not to fall into the habit, as some good brethren have, of mentioning the same things time after time, and only those things. Of course it is good to say, "We thank thee for this beautiful day," and "Bless the sick and afflicted." But, if we say a few things like these every time, and by so doing crowd out of the prayer other things that need to be included, then that's not the best way to pray.

Situations differ from week to week and day to day. Stop and think about the present situation. Is there something about it that should be included in your prayer? Are you beginning a new series of Bible lessons? Is a new teacher about to present his first lesson? Is a personal evangelism program being planned? Some of the things that are often forgotten in this prayer and the "main" prayer in the assembly of the church are: Our missionaries, the lost people of the community, our elders, our preachers, our senior citizens, our youth, the rulers of the world, the poor, the troubled, the widows and the orphans.

## *Exercise*

1.   Copy three verses from the Psalms which give words of praise or thanksgiving that may be used appropriately today in our prayers.

2.   Copy three statements of praise or thanksgiving found in Bible prayers, other than in the Psalms.

3.   Write down five petitions which you think would be suitable for the "main" prayer, and which would be sufficient for such a prayer. Fix these five subjects in your mind, and when you are called on to lead the prayer, make these petitions without having memorized the exact words to be used. Don't wait until someone remembers to call on you for prayer; but when you gain the courage to undertake it, go to one of the elders and tell him you are ready to lead the prayer as soon as you are needed for it. "Get your feet wet," then go back and study this section again. Also review chapters II, III, and VI. You will see ways in which you can improve and do a little better next time.

### *Samples of the "Main" Prayer in the Assembly*

"Our Father and our God, in whom we live, move and have our being. We approach thy throne of grace this morning with thankful hearts; thanking thee for the many blessings of this life, both spiritual and material. Heavenly Father, we are so thankful for the privilege of coming together as Christians to worship thee, the true and living God. We are thankful, Heavenly Father, for each and every individual here this morning.

"Bless all whom it is our duty to pray for the world over, especially those that are of the household of faith.

"Above all, our Heavenly Father, are we thankful for thy Son Jesus who suffered and died, that we might in and through him and in obedience to his commands, have eternal life.

"Heavenly Father, we would ask thee to be with our preacher as he brings the message. Be with each of us as listeners. We would ask thee, Heavenly Father, to look down upon us and forgive us of anything we may have said, done or thought contrary to thy holy word, that we might stand justified in thy sight once more.

"We would ask a special blessing, Heavenly Father, on those who are sick or bereaved. May the things being done for the sick restore them to their health if it be thy will. If not, be with them in their suffering.

"We would ask thee, Heavenly Father, to be with us now in the remainder of this service. Go with us on down through the uneven journeys of this life. Be with us in the things that are right; defeat us in the things that are wrong. And when we can be here no longer by reason of death, hand us down to our graves in peace with all mankind; own us and crown us, and give us a home with thee in heaven.

"These favors and blessings we ask in Christ's name. Amen."

—J.H. Vinson

Note: the following are group (of public) prayers and references to such prayers.

Numbers 6:23-26; 2 Chronicles 20:5-12; Ezra 8:21-23; Acts 1:24, 25; 4:23-30; 6:6; 12:12; 13:3; 20:36,37; 21:5; Ephesians 3:14-21; 1 Timothy 2:8; Revelation 5:13, 14.

## *Example of a Prayer at the Beginning of a Bible Class*

"Great God. Our Father in Heaven. Hallowed be your name. Our hearts are filled with praise and thanksgiving when we consider what it means that you have revealed yourself to man. We humbly thank you for your word, the Bible, and for the opportunity we have at this time of coming here to study your word together.

"Bless, we pray, the one who will be leading us in this study; and bless us all that we may gain a better understanding of the truth. Also that we may apply it, each of us to his own life; and that we may be better Christians as a result of this study.

"Bless, with us, we pray, Father, the other classes being conducted here. Also, may the service that follows this have thy richest blessings.

"Father, again we thank thee for Jesus, our Savior; and in his name we offer this prayer. Amen."

(Note: The prayer could be shortened somewhat. Also other matters could be included. And should the Bible class be in the home of a lost person, you surely would want to include a request that God's blessings be on the home where you are meeting.)

## *Story of a Fitting Prayer*

On this day 495 Christians had assembled for a special thanksgiving and praise service. It was truly a cosmopolitan group. There were rich people and poor. People sick and well. Whole and crippled. Hungry and well fed. People free of troubles and people who were not, including some who were mourning the passing of loved ones. The lonely and those with families and friends were there. The homeless and the well housed. Also a few visitors from foreign lands; even from Communist countries.

The service started with a prayer led by one of the bishops. This was followed by a hymn of praise. Every song was to be of that nature and each was to follow a prayer of thanksgiving.

The first prayer had in it little that was specific. It was a general prayer of thanksgiving and praise. Everyone said Amen when it was finished and sang the song which followed with gusto. It was inspiring.

The second brother to lead in prayer said, "We thank thee and praise thee, O God our Father in heaven, for the political freedom we enjoy, that we can assemble like this without fear of molestation from the authorities. And we are grateful that we can live in peace."

Eighteen good people, visitors from Communist and/or war-torn countries, had to drop out of the Amens and the hymn that followed.

Then another brother went to the microphone and led a prayer, thanking the Lord for "the prosperity which we enjoy, for our good jobs and for the comfortable houses we have in which to live." The Amens at the end of this prayer were not nearly so loud, and the song which they sang did not sound as good as usual. The poor could not enter into these things. Neither could the unemployed nor the homeless. Not even the people who resided under crowded and poor housing conditions. About 150 people were left out and even made to feel uncomfortable.

So the evening wore on with other leaders saying prayers which failed to fit all the congregation. Until finally, an old brother arose and asked to lead a prayer. His prayer was this, "We offer thee, O God, the sincere gratitude of our hearts for thyself. For thy great love. Especially for the priceless gift of thine only beloved son, our Savior. In his name we humbly pray. Amen."

He did not say that Amen alone. Every Christian there joined him in it; and they all sang the song that followed with gusto. Almost as soon as the hymn began, a brother on the front row struggled to his feet, with the help of his crutches. Seeing him, others began to stand to sing. Soon everyone was on his feet, and the sound of that song echoed from wall to wall.

At last a prayer had been led which fitted the whole group. At last they had a prayer leader who had given some thought to the situation and to the conditions of the people present, before he got up to lead.

# CHAPTER SEVEN

# How to Work Out the Wording for Various Prayers

## SECTION 3

### 1. Prayers at the Communion Table

On the night of his betrayal, Jesus instituted the Lord's Supper (also called communion or the breaking of bread). See Matthew 26; Mark 14; Luke 22; 1 Corinthians 10; 1 Corinthians 11. The Lord command his disciples to *(1)* do this, and *(2)* do it in memory of him. The early Christians, under the teaching of the apostles of Christ, met together on the first day of the week for the purpose of breaking bread, as we see from Acts 20:7. This was the primary purpose for the Sunday meetings of the church then, and should continue to be the primary purpose of Sunday meetings today.

In instituting this memorial, Jesus gave thanks before passing the bread and again before passing the fruit of the vine. Such also was the practice of the church after he went back to heaven (1 Corinthians 10:16).

Before we can know how to lead these two prayer, we must understand what they are. They are prayers of thanksgiving. They are not petitions for God to bless the loaf and the cup. They are prayers of thanksgiving. Some are confused at this point, because in two places it says Jesus took the bread and "blessed" and gave it to them. This doesn't mean he asked the Father to bless the bread. Nor does it mean in this case that Jesus pronounced his blessings upon the bread. The verb "blessed," both in the English and the original language, sometimes has this meaning; but not always. At times "blessed" simply means to give thanks. When Jesus fed the 5,000, it is said he took the food and "blessed"; but when he fed the 4,000 it is said he "gave thanks" (Matthew 14:19 and 15:36). Surely he did the same thing on both occasions. He gave thanks. God created our meat to be received "with thanksgiving" (1 Timothy 4:3). Evidently Jesus was doing this when he took the food and "blessed," as recorded in Matthew 14.

Of the four accounts of the institution of the Lord's Supper, two in the King James version read that Jesus tood bread and "blessed," and the other two read the he "gave thanks." Thus, "blessed" and "gave thanks" are used interchangeably. What one means, the other means. In none of these four places does the Bible say that Jesus "blessed" the cup. We are simply told that he "gave thanks." It is evident that "blessed" and "gave thanks" in these passages mean the same thing.

What Jesus did when he instituted the Lord's Supper:

|  | TAKING BREAD | TAKING THE CUP |
|---|---|---|
| Matt. 26:26,27 | Blessed | Gave thanks |
| Mark 14:22,23 | Blessed | Gave thanks |
| Luke 22:19,20 | Gave thanks | "Likewise" (gave thanks) |
| 1 Cor. 11:24,25 | Gave thanks | "After the same manner" (gave thanks) |

We cannot object to the idea of our consecrating the bread and the cup. Even our daily food, for which we give thanks, is consecrated by the word of God and prayer (1 Timothy 4:4,5). But to consecrate the bread and wine would not be enough. Christ offered thanks. We should do so too.

These are prayers of thanksgiving. If a brother chooses to ask God's blessings on the bread or cup, he has not sinned; but neither has he given thanks. He would need to also give thanks.

For what are you to give thanks in these prayers at the Lord's table? You need a clear understanding of what it is. Are these prayers for the purpose of expressing gratitude that "our lives have been spared," or "for this beautiful day." Obviously not. It isn't wrong to be thankful for such things at any time. But these things do not need to be mentioned at the time of the Lord's Supper. Everyone's thoughts should be focused on the Lord and his sacrifice for our sins. This is what we should be giving thanks for. The communion bread represents the body of Christ, given for us at Calvary; and the cup represents the shed blood. Thus to eat the bread and drink the cup is to "shew the Lord's death till he come" (1 Corinthians 11:26). Surely, then, our thoughts and our prayers of thanksgiving during the communion are to be centered on the death of Christ.

While this is true, yet the Lord's words were not, "Do this in remembrance of my death." He said, "Do this in remembrance of me" (1 Corinthians 11:24, 25). We don't just remember his death. We remember the Lord, who died. We remember the personality and character of Christ, as well as what he did at Calvary. He said, "in remembrance of me." These things cannot be separated from the event of his death. The radius of our thanksgiving takes in the other things he did to bring about our salvation.

In this connection, the following article may be helpful. It was first printed in a newspaper in Poughkeepsie, NY in 1983.

## DEATH AND RESURRECTION

The death, burial, and resurrection of Christ is the very heart of the gospel. "Moreover, brethren, I declare unto you the gospel . . . how that Christ died for our sins according to the Scriptures; and that he was buried, and that he arose again . . . " (1 Corinthians 15:1-4).

Moreover, the Lord has left us a memorial of his death and resurrection. It is not Easter. The word, Easter, appears one time in the Bible and only in the KJ Version: Acts 12:4, where it obviously refers to a Jewish festival, rather than a Christian one. The revised version shows that the occasion was the Passover, or "days of unleavened bread." Neither do we find in the Bible the words: Lent, Palm Sunday, Ash Wednesday, or Good Friday. History reveals that the Easter celebration began in the second century, which was after the Bible had been completed. See Mosheim's Ecclesiastical History, Vol, P. 135, 5th ed.

The Biblical memorial of the death and resurrection of our Lord is called the Lord's Supper, the Breaking of Bread and the Communion (1 Corinthians 1:20-25 and 10:16, Acts 2:42 and 20:7). Acts 20:7 shows this memorial was observed on a weekly occasion (first day or the week, our Sunday).

The elements of the Lord's Supper (unleavened bread and fruit of the vine) represent the sacrificed body of Christ and his shed blood. See Matthew 26; Mark 14; Luke 22 and 1 Corinthians 11. Therefore, the Communion is a celebration of the death of Christ. It goes beyond that, however. Instead of saying, "do this in memory of my death," Jesus said, "do this in memory of me." It is to be done in memory of the person, with his death as the pivot point. His death would be meaningless without his resurrection. In the Communion, we remember the broken body and shed blood of the LIVING Saviour. We remember the one who "was dead" and is "alive for evermore" (Revelation 1:18). The atonement was not completed at the point of his death. Jesus "was delivered up for our trespasses and raised for our justification" (Romans 4:25).

It's significant that the Bible gives a memorial celebration; and gives only one. Also that it's a weekly celebration; not an annual one. Why are people not concerned to observe the Bible celebration? Why substitute something not authorized by Scripture?

On the other hand, why do some people oppose the unbiblical feast and are content to remain negative, not observing the weekly feast of the Bible?

At the communion table, we center our thoughts on the atoning death of our Lord; but in our peripheral vision we take in these other things. We remember him. We give thanks for him. For him who suffered and died that we might live. Perhaps we could say that we are remembering him directly in his death, and indirectly we are remembering him in other things. It is significant that the Lord gave his disciples no separate memorials of his birth nor of his resurrection. The religious celebration of Christmas and Easter are not of Bible origin. Christ only gave us the Lord's Supper.

The things said in the last two paragraphs are not intended to mar the simplicity of the Lord's Supper. Surely it is not essential that we parade before the mind's eye a specific list of the acts and attributes of Christ while eating the bread and drinking the cup. However, we should remember him ("in remembrance of me") and not think of his death as an isolated thing or as the only thing to remember and appreciate about him.

Turning to something else, now, let me suggest that instead of including the statement commonly made, "Help each of us to do this in an acceptable manner," it is better to be more specific and say something like this, "Help each one to be thinking about Christ and his death, as we partake."

These prayers do not seem to be the kind that require long introductions of praise. Not all prayers do. We note that the prayers Jesus prayed on the cross did not contain such introductions. He simply said, "Father, forgive them, for they know not what they do"; and "Father, into thy hands I commend my spirit." Many Bible prayers are brief like this. Yet a brief statement of praise to God usually is helpful in the communion prayers. It makes it easier for us to get into an attitude of reverence and gratitude.

## Samples of Communion Prayers

After speaking a few short words of praise to God, you could say something like this: "We thank thee for the living Christ, who gave his body as a sacrifice for our sins. Help us to partake of this bread in remembrance of him. In his name. Amen." Or, "We thank thee for Jesus who came to this world to save us, who lived such a beautiful life and died so willingly for our sins; who arose from the dead and is at thy right hand today, making intercession for us. As we eat of this bread help us to center our thoughts upon Calvary, and to be thankful. In Christ's name. Amen."

Something similar can be said when you take the cup.

At the end of the chapter are some communion prayers suggested by or prayed by others. Study them for what ideas they may give you, then form your own prayers. Avoid borrowing too heavily from the wording of someone else.

## 2. Praying at Contribution Time

It is a common practice to have a public prayer before the collection plates are passed. It's good practice, but should not be thought of as a ritual requirement. Surely every contributor ought to be prayerful when giving; and it is good for the congregation to pray together. This prayer could be either before or after the plates have been passed. After the collection comes in, it would be well to pray in the same way and to add a "thank you" for the moneys received that the church may do her work more effectively.

This is a good time to tell the Lord again how thankful we are for his material blessings.

Praying that the Lord will accept our offerings is especially important when we come to make our contributions. If the prayer leader doesn't mention it, each of us should make this request under his breath. Why? Because giving is not just "kicking in our share." It's worship. Its type is found in the sacrifices and offerings made by Old Testament people. "To do good and to communicate, forget not: for with such sacrifices God is well pleased" (Hebrews 13:16). We, as a holy priesthood, "offer up spiritual sacrifices, acceptable to God by Jesus Christ" (1 Peter 2:5). Our giving is one of those sacrifices, and we are concerned that it be acceptable to God. Thus we want to ask him to accept our gift. A gift made for the support of a gospel preacher was called by Paul, "a sacrifice acceptable, well-pleasing to God" (Philippians 4:18). We should always be concerned that our gifts be sacrifices acceptable, well-pleasing to God. This, we want to pray about. We don't want to be like Cain, whose offering was rejected.

First, make every effort to give in an acceptable way. The gift should be offered by faith. We should make the gift both cheerfully and bountifully. See Hebrews 11:4, 2 Corinthians 9:6,7. We should offer it to the Lord, asking him to please accept it. Our gift should always be liberal enough that we need not to be ashamed to ask God to accept it.

With our monetary gift, we are to give ourselves. Paul praised the liberality of the churches in Macedonia. He said, ". . . In a great trial of affliction the abundance of their joy and their deep poverty abounded unto the riches of their liberality"; and he went on to say that they "first gave their own selves to the Lord and unto us by the will of God" (2 Corinthians 8:1-5). Their example is commended to us. And this kind of giving makes the contribution an important act of worship. It needs to be done with prayer.

Often I hear brethren pray, "Help us to give cheerfully." Not very often do I hear anyone pray, "Help us to give liberally." Yet bountiful giving and cheerful giving are mentioned together (2 Corinthians 9:6,7).

Often I hear the brethren pray, "May the money be used Scripturally and wisely by the elders of the church." Not very often do I hear anyone pray, "Help us to use what we keep back in a Scriptural and wise way."

I am a little worried about these things. Are brethren more interested in being cheerful than in being liberal? Are they more concerned about the stewardship of the elders than about their own stewardship? Perhaps it is a matter of thoughtfulness. Let us think about what we say in prayer.

### *Exercise*

1.   Without copying the phrases of another, write one prayer suitable for use at each of these occasions: (1) Before the communion bread is eaten, (2) Before the cup is taken, and (3) Before the collection is taken.

2.   Give two different definitions of the verb, "to bless."

3. True or False? In instituting the Lord's Supper, Jesus said, "Do this in memory of my death."

4. Write down one thing you think should be in every prayer at contribution time.

5. Examine the prayer in 1 Chronicles 29:10-19 and indicate something we may learn from it about our prayers in connection with the contribution.

## *Samples of Communion Prayers - The Bread*

"We praise your name, Lord, for what this bread means to us. Help each one that partakes of this bread to center his mind, not only on Jesus' sacrifice for us, but on his life. May our lives become more like his each day; for through his name we pray. Amen."

--Greg Foster

"Our Father in Heaven, Ruler of all nature, we praise thy great name. Father, we give thee thanks for this opportunity we have to assemble this Lord's day to worship thee and observe the Lord's Supper, remembering the great sacrifice that was made for us. As we prepare to partake of this bread, symbolic of our Lord's body, may we remember that sacrifice, and put aside worldly matters and dwell on spiritual things, so that we may be closer to thee. Now may we partake in a pleasing manner to thee, as we pray that our sins will be forgiven. In the name of Jesus our Savior, we pray. Amen."

--Dalton Driver

"Our most gracious and heavenly Father; we are most thankful for this day that is set aside that we may gather here to worship you, and especially to commemorate the death and suffering of your own beloved Son and our Saviour, Jesus Christ. Heavenly Father, we are thankful also for his love, that he was willing to come to this earth and suffer and die at the hands of those he came to save. We thank you, Father, that through his death we have the opportunity to receive the forgiveness of our sins. We pray, Father, that as we partake of this emblem which represents his body that he gave on that cross, that we may do so in a way that will bring honor and glory to your holy name. For we ask it all in Christ's name. Amen."

--Bobby Paul Hord

## *Samples of Communion Prayers - The Fruit of the Vine*

"Our Heavenly Father: again we come to you, thanking you for all our wonderful blessings that you have bestowed upon us. And at this time we ask that you bless and be with us and help us to put all worldly thoughts from our minds and think only of that day when our Lord and Savior suffered and died on the cross for our sins. Be with us as we now partake of this fruit of the vine, for we do this in remembrance of your Son. These things we ask in the name of our Lord and Savior, Jesus Christ. Amen."

--Joe Reeves

"Heavenly Father, we praise your name. We especially thank you for what this fruit of the vine represents. Without your Son's sacrifice and shed blood we would have no hope of salvation. Help us to live a life that is a living sacrifice to you for we pray through Jesus. Amen."

--Greg Foster

## *Samples of Contribution Prayers*

"Our Heavenly Father: again we are thankful for this first day of the week. We thank thee our Heavenly Father, that we have this privilege of giving, that we might give back to thee as we have prospered. We ask this in Christ's name. Amen."

--Joe Bob Vinson

Gracious Heavenly Father, we recognize that all we have is from you, and that it is of your own money that we give to you at this time. Help us to give bountifully and cheerfully, according to that which we have purposed to give. And please accept our offerings. In Jesus holy name. Amen.

# CHAPTER SEVEN
# How to Work Out the Wording for Various Prayers

## SECTION 4

### *Praying When a Brother Comes Forward to Confess His Sins*

Christians not only have the privilege of confessing their sins to God and asking for forgiveness (1 John 1:9), but also the privilege of confessing their sins "one to another" (James 5:16). This is not only because we are brothers and sisters in the Lord, but because every Christian is a priest (Revelation 1:6). The New Testament doesn't recognize a special priesthood among Christians. There's no special class of people to whom you need to confess your sins. As a priest you may go to God on your own. You may also solicit the prayers of other priests (Christians). Simon asked Peter to pray for him (Acts 8:24).

There are times when one needs to confess his sins publicly, because his sins are known by the public. Frequently brethren come forward during the invitation song to confess sins and be restored to the Lord's favor. When this happens, it seems important to me that the congregation have a prayer with him. He is important and deserves that we take time for such a prayer. If you are called on to lead a prayer like this, what will you say? A little thought will indicate that the main thing is to ask for God's pardon for him. Also that he may have God's strength. I have known of times when the prayer-leader left out these things. I have heard something like this said, "Thank you, Lord, for the one who has come forward and for his courage." If this is all that is said, it sounds like the person is a model Christian and doesn't really need forgiveness. Surely what he desires is for you to join him in praying for God's forgiveness and help.

The prayer doesn't need to be long; and it shouldn't be. It is not a general prayer. It is for one special purpose.

After speaking a few words of praise to the Lord's name, you could say something like this: "We join with our Brother Williams in asking that you look down on him with mercy and forgive him. May he leave this service with the assurance you have forgiven him, remembering your promise that if we confess our sins, you will forgive us. May he be encouraged by this assurance. Keep him strong as he goes about serving you from day to day. Help us to encourage him and to assist him in every way we can. In Jesus' name. Amen."

### *Praying With One Who Has Just Been Baptized*

Our Lord prayed when he was baptized (Luke 3:21). According to Galatians 3:26,27 at that time one becomes a child of God, and so is on praying terms with God. He should be encouraged to begin communing with his Heavenly Father immediately. Have a prayer with him. If you happen to be the baptist, the prayer could be said just after you raise him from the watery grave, while you both are still in the pool. It could be said in the dressing room. If the congregation waits for him to dress, the prayer could be said as soon as you and he come back out of the dressing room. If it is a small crowd that is waiting, it is nice for the people to form a circle and hold hands for the prayer.

If you are not the one who administers the baptism, it is still possible that you will be asked to lead this prayer. So be ready. And when you get ready, let someone know he can call on you.

What would be in order for such a prayer? Certainly it would be proper to begin with words of praise and thanksgiving to the Lord who has made all this possible. You might thank him for his grace, the gift of his Son, the power of his word. For the privilege of having heard the name of Christ confessed and having seen one buried with his Lord in baptism. Thank God that according to his promise, the person has been forgiven of all past sins and adopted into God's family, the blood-bought church. Pray for the spiritual welfare of this new babe in Christ. These things would surely be in order and there are other things that could be included.

## Meeting a Request to Have a Special Prayer

It may be that someone is critically ill and one of his loved ones has requested a special prayer. It may be some crisis which is threatening (like war), or has happened (like an earthquake). It may be some individual has made the request to the elders, or it may be the elders have decided to have a special prayer. It may be a missionary family is about to leave the community for a field of labor. Perhaps there is an important program of work facing the church. There could be any number of occasions for a special prayer. While the matter may be included in the regular prayers, it still would be in order to have a prayer especially for this.

Our image should be such that people of the community will feel free to request special prayers when they face troubles, like a critical illness. Let us be known as a church that believes in praying and that is interested in the welfare of other people. There's nothing wrong in advertising our willingness to pray for the sick of the community. People should be told that simply because we believe miraculous healing was for a special purpose in the formative stage of the church, it doesn't follow that we doubt the value of prayer. We can pray for the sick to recover if it be according to God's will, and many such prayers are granted.

What you say in this kind of prayer depends mostly on the nature of the problem about which you are requested to pray. The primary difference between this kind and a general prayer is that you have more time to talk about the one problem. Acts 4:23-30 gives such a prayer. Persecution had just broken out; and the brethren were concerned, not so much about the prospect of suffering, but about the danger of their becoming fearful and failing to preach the gospel with boldness. This one thing is what they prayed about, after starting out with many words of praise to the Lord. Study this prayer.

If a hurricane has hit the coast of some land, bringing devastation, you could first offer words of praise to the Lord then say something like this: "We earnestly pray for the people effected by the hurricane. And we pray for those who are mourning the loss of loved ones because of this storm. Bless them as only thou art able. Lessen their troubles and sorrows, if it be in keeping with thy righteous will. As the storm advances inland, we pray that the lives of the people will be spared, if possible. Father, our prayers are especially for members of the household of faith who have been effected by this storm. Be with each one. Bless him and keep him in the hollow of thy hand. May we not forget to pray for all these people in our private prayers. Open our hearts that we may be willing to send relief to the disaster area if it is needed. In the precious name of Christ. Amen."

The same principles can be adopted when praying for different problems, such as sickness. And as you think through these things, you will be able to form a prayer that will be satisfying both to all who join with you in praying and to the Lord who hears your petition.

We have great opportunity to do good by our praying and ought not to neglect it.

Welcome the requests for special prayers and learn how to pray them well.

## *The Closing Prayer*

Stop and ask. What is the purpose of this prayer? It is sometimes called the dismissal or the benediction. That is, it invokes God's blessings on the people as they depart to go their separate ways. Such is its simple purpose. This tells us that the prayer can be short. It should also enable us to understand what the general contents of the benediction should be. By this time we have already had a certain number of prayers together; and now it is time to call down God's benedictions on us as we leave the assembly.

You could say this, "Dear God, be with us 'till we meet again. In Jesus' name. Amen." This would do. However, it is better to say a little more than this, most of us feel. We don't want to sound like we are rushing to get out the door, so we can be first in line at the local cafeteria. And there are some things that need to be said in this prayer. If there is something on the people's mind, such as a special meeting that's coming soon or if there is a brother who is seriously ill, it would be well to include something about it. And as we are about to close the service, surely we should feel grateful for having been there. We can well thank God for this privilege. Shouldn't we ask the Lord to help us go out and serve him and to put into practice the things we have learned in the meeting and to act upon the good inspirations of the hour? Surely, some of these things should be mentioned in the dismissal.

## *Exercise*

1.  Is it proper to "go to confessional" (confess sins to one of a priestly class in some religious group)? Write out your reasons for approving or objecting to this practice and give Scriptures to back up your statements.

2.  Write out a suitable prayer for use in the event you were called on to lead when (1) a brother comes forward confessing his sins, (2) one has just been baptized, (3) when the request has been made for a special prayer in behalf of Mr. Doe who is critically ill, and (4) for a dismissal prayer at the end of a Sunday morning service.

3.  Immediately following the baptism of an individual, would it be wise to ask him to say a prayer? Give your thoughts on the subject.

## *Sample of the Benediction*

"All righteous and wise God, our Father, we are thankful for this day, for the Lord's day; for the occasion that brings us together this evening. We are thankful for the church and for Jesus Christ who died and shed his blood to purchase it. We are thankful for the preaching of your word at this time. For the power of your word, and for the work it can do through us. We pray that you will help us as we go forth from this assembly to be examples to others and to let your will be done in our lives. We pray for the church at this place. We pray for the meeting that's in progress. Continue to bless Brother Banister in the proclamation. We pray for the local preacher and the elders, and each member of the congregation. We ask you now to go with us as we separate, and help us to be a blessing to those around us. In Jesus' name. Amen."

--Anthony Bryant

# CHAPTER SEVEN

# How to Work Out the Wording for Various Prayers

## SECTION 5

### Some Prayers Outside the Assembly of the Church

*1. PRAYING BESIDE THE BED OF A SICK PERSON.* If this prayer is not long and tiring, or if what is said is not upsetting, it can mean much to the one who is ill. When a preacher makes hospital calls, the usual thing is for him to have a prayer in the rooms where he visits. It is generally expected that he will do so. If the preacher just visits and leaves a room without giving the patient opportunity to ask for his prayers, the patient is likely to think he doesn't believe in prayer. Or he may think the preacher doesn't pray for people who are not of his faith, should the patient be of a different religion.

Personally, I don't always ask the person if he wants me to say a prayer. Not always. In many cases, to avoid what might embarrass the patient, I simply ask, What can I do for you? In response to this question, he may request an interest in my prayers. Usually, I can tell from what he says and the way he says it, whether it would upset him for me to say a prayer at that time. I may ask, "Would you like for me to have a prayer now?" Try not to upset the patient. If you do that a few times, the word will get around and people will dread to see you coming. So will the doctors and nurses.

In most cases you will be able to pray in the sick room. You should seek such opportunities. Whether or not the sick person is a Christian, good will come. A close friend of mine, Howard Swinney, did much good this way, when he was preaching in Anson, Texas. He told me that in many cases, he would simply say, "Let's have a prayer." His hospital visitation resulted in a number of people being led to Christ. Hospital visitation is an opportunity and an important part of it is the prayer by the bedside of the sick.

It is not just for preachers to pray by the sick bed. This practice should be more general among Christians.

Good judgement should be used in what you say in these prayers. Even more so when the sick person is not a Christian. Start by offering a few words of praise and thanksgiving. Even the seriously ill have much to be thankful for. Such things as family and friends, medical science and hospitals, the blessings of past life, etc.

You can always thank God for Jesus Christ.

Pray that God may bless this person in his infirmity and bless the treatment he is receiving. Ask the Lord to guide the hand of the surgeon, if an operation is scheduled. You may pray for a speedy recovery "if it be God's will." If the disease has been pronounced terminal, be very careful what you say about recovery. Ask for the gift of patience for the sick person. Ask for ease from his pain. Pray that all of us may have spiritual health above other things. If the person is a Christian, ask the Lord to "forgive us our sins." If he is not a Christian, he will not experience the new birth while in bed as you pray with him. There is more than that to becoming a Child of God. See Matthew 7:21-23; Mark 16:16; John 3:3-5; Romans 6:3, 4, 17, 18; Acts 2:38 and 22:16; Galatians 3:26, 27 and 1 Peter 3:21, etc. Read these verses from your own Bible and don't make the mistake of holding out a false hope to the man in bed.

If you have reason to believe the infirm man is not on praying terms with God, that doesn't prevent you from praying. You can not pray with him; but you can pray for him.

You are not likely to make a serious blunder if you love people genuinely and are humble and sincere in what you say and thoughtful about the way you say it. Just pray silently before you enter the sick room, asking the Lord to help you do good and not harm. Pray in faith. Then all will be well.

2. *PRAYING WITH THE SURVIVORS WHEN SOME-ONE HAS DIED.* Let's say you have just heard about a death and are disposed to go to the home of the family to show your concern. Should you offer to have a prayer with them? If so, what should you say?

Don't force your prayers on to a bereaved family. Some of them may feel that a formal prayer would be too much of a strain on them at the moment. Try to size up the situation. Sometimes you would want to say, "I'll be praying for you; may God bless you." It would be wise to simply say something like this if the people are not very religious. However, in many instances, it will do much good for you to have a short prayer with the family.

"Short" is a key word in this situation, I believe. Make the prayer short.

Be sure you sound kind. Avoid saying anything that might stir up greater grief. It isn't time to dwell on the sadness of the hour. And it isn't time to preach to someone in your prayer. If perhaps the deceased was not a Christian and died quickly, you can thank the Lord he did not suffer long. You can express thanks for his having lived as long as he has. For the blessings that have come out of this life, and for the precious memories that remain.

You can always ask God to care for those who grieve. To give them comfort and strength, both for this hour of sorrow and for the days ahead.

If the deceased was a faithful Christian, you can praise God for the hope which the survivors have for him. If it is evident the man was not prepared to die, it is probably better to say nothing about his condition. You can't afford to lie about it just to comfort the bereaved. If you want to, you can say something like this: "Father, we are thankful to know that when any of us departs this life, he is in the hands of a just and merciful God."

Scripturally, you cannot pray for the dead. Once a person has passed over the river of death, he is beyond the reach of anything we can do for him. Regardless of the way he lived, he has no further need of anything we can supply. It is not proper for us to ask God to have mercy on his soul. Not that we are unconcerned. But God does not need our prayers for this thing, and He has not asked for them. Men's only time for preparation to meet God is in this life. After it is over for a man, we cannot help him make further preparation. He will be judged according to the deeds done in his body (2 Corinthians 5:10). If there is any reason for clemency in an individual's case, the Great Judge will know it. We do not have to tell him.

If we could help the dead by our prayers, we would need to devote a great percentage of our waking hours praying for all the dead of the world. Especially for those who died in a lost condition. We would have little time for trying to win the living to Christ. If our prayers could benefit the souls of the departed, surely the Lord would have placed in the Great Commission a charge to pray for the dead. Instead, he charged us to preach to the living. It has "pleased God by the foolishness of preaching to save them that believe" (1 Corinthians 1:21). The only way we can save a lost soul is by the power of the gospel, as we preach to him.

The dead do not need our prayers; but the living do. We need to pray for one another while we live.

Praying with people who have just lost a loved one is not exactly easy. But just think about it first and seek the Lord's help. Ask for wisdom (James 1:5). You will do all right.

Most of the things which apply to praying in the home of survivors will apply to praying at a funeral service, in event you have occasion to lead in such prayers.

3. *PRAYING AT COMMUNITY GATHERINGS, CIVIC CLUB MEETINGS, ETC.* I see no reason why you should not say a prayer at such a gathering if you are asked to do so. But, in thinking about how to word the prayer, there are certain things you would want to consider. Likely the group is not just made up of Christians. You don't want to leave the impression that every person, regardless of his religion or of his life, is on praying terms with God. Most people think they are; but this is not Bible teaching. Read 1 Peter 3:12; Proverbs 15:8, 29; Isaiah 59:2; Matthew 7:21.

You could just pray in the first person singular (as people are accustomed to hearing some preachers do). In this way, you are not leading the people in prayer, but are praying for them in public. You could say something like this: "Heavenly Father, hallowed be thy name. Thou art the true and living God, and the father of Jesus Christ, the Savior. I come to thee, in his precious name, to offer thanks for this community and for the community-spirit which is evidenced by this meeting today. I thank thee for the spirit of such clubs as this one and for the good they have done in the community. Bless the deliberations here today. Give wisdom to the leaders of the group. Father, may your blessings be not only upon the meeting, but upon each person present. Also upon each family represented. Bless our community; and bless our nation. For I pray in the name of Jesus Christ. Amen."

Some of the things you could mention, besides those given in the prayer above, are our children and our schools, those who are sick or poor, the bereaved and the troubled, etc. You could express thanks to God for any number of blessings.

It is sincerely hoped you will never be ashamed to say that you are praying in the name of Jesus Christ, even in the presence of Jews, Muslims, and others who reject our Lord. The Lord said, "Whosoever therefore shall be ashamed of me and of my words in this adulterous and sinful generation; of him also shall the Son of man be ashamed, when he cometh in the glory of his Father with the holy angels" (Mark 8:38).

*4. IF CALLED ON TO PRAY AT A SECTARIAN ASSEMBLY.* The Christian believes in praying. He can pray anywhere, any time. However, this is not the same as saying he can lead anybody in prayer at any time.

If you were a visitor at a religious service where the things being done and taught are unscriptural, and you were asked to lead in a prayer, should you do so? The first fact to consider is that you cannot be party to something that is wrong in God's sight. "And have no fellowship with the unfruitful works of darkness, but rather reprove them" (Ephesians 5:11). You could pray; but you could not afford to lead their prayer for them; to help them conduct a part of their worship service. To avoid this, you might say, when requested to lead this prayer, "Excuse me, please." Maybe adding, "Please allow me to just visit and listen respectfully and learn all I can." However, perhaps it's possible for you to say a prayer at such a meeting without participating in their worship or condoning the things they do and teach. It may be you can pray, without leading them in their prayer; pray for them without praying with them. I say, perhaps you can. It is a decision for you to make. Such a prayer would have to be different from one you would pray when leading the minds of fellow Christians in a scriptural situation. What differences would there be? Would the prayer be such as to antagonize the people? Should they be antagonized in this way? Would it do good or harm? These are questions you would need to settle before undertaking to say the prayer.

If you decide to pray at a meeting which you consider to be unscriptural or which promotes something unscriptural, you might pray in the first person singular and say something like this: "Lord, God of heaven and earth; the Christian's heavenly Father. It is in the name of the Lord Jesus Christ, the world's only hope, that I make this prayer; thanking you first of all for Jesus who came to this earth, suffered and died to provide salvation for the lost. And, Lord, I thank you that my friends here have been kind enough to ask me to pray. Will you bless each one who is here today and each home which is represented. Will you bless our nation. and preserve the freedom we enjoy in America. Bless our community too. Especially bless the sick and the poor and the troubled. Bless us all in our search for a better understanding of your word and a willingness to recognize Jesus as the Christ, the Son of the living God. Help every earnest soul as he searches the Scriptures for light. Help us all to love the truth, lest we should receive a working of error and be damned because we love not the truth, as Paul once said. We have honest differences in our religion, and I pray you will help us to respect one another's convictions, and to study together and work for the kind of unity for which the Lord prayed in his great intercessory prayer. Now, Lord, I pray that your will may be done in the lives of all of us; that you will encourage us in the things which are right and scriptural and defeat us in the things that are wrong. For I make this prayer humbly in the precious name of Jesus. Amen."

You want the prayer to be long enough to sound like a proper prayer; and you want to be very careful how you word it. You should have thought this through before going to the meeting and have it well worked out. Don't be unnecessarily offensive; but have the courage to pray without giving endorsement to the things being done there. You can pray for the individuals present, without praying God's blessings upon the meeting and the program of the hour. You can be positive in your statements rather than negative; and careful to leave out the statements which would give endorsement to the message or the organization. Three words to remember are, careful, careful, careful. A phrase to remember is, Be very humble.

Some gospel preachers I know never refuse to lead a prayer when asked to do so, regardless of the unscriptural nature of the meeting. Personally, when faced with this situation, I have always kindly requested to be excused. However, if I had it to do over, there is one situation in which I would say the prayer. It was while living and preaching in old Hot Springs, New Mexico, that I visited a sectarian service, and the pastor of that church called on me to lead the first prayer, without consulting me about it privately. I said, "Please excuse me." Then at the end of the service he called on me to lead the dismissal. Again I excused myself. I'll always feel he was deliberately trying to embarrass me, by calling on me the second time in the same service. The next time something like this happens, I'll say that second prayer. After speaking a word of praise, I think I will say something like this: "Lord, I thank thee for the freedoms we enjoy in this great nation, including the freedom to worship according to our beliefs, without being afraid of persecution. I am thankful that most people respect the convictions of others who differ from them, and that we can all be good neighbors and love one another. I thank thee, Lord, that I have been called on to pray at this place, and to ask thy blessings on everybody, as we leave here. We all need thee. Wilt thou bless each one as thou seest his needs and in accordance with thy righteous will. For I pray in the precious name of Jesus Christ. Amen."

## *Exercise*

1.  Write down three things in each of the following prayers for which it would be fitting to offer thanks: (1) A prayer beside the bed of a sick person; (2) A prayer with a bereaved family.

2.  Write down three requests that would be proper to make in each of the above named prayers.

3.  Write a paragraph giving Bible reasons for not praying for the dead.

4.  By thumbing back through this book, find and write down the number of the chapter which deals with the subject of whether or not a lost sinner is on praying terms with God. Also give page numbers where this matter is discussed.

## *Examples of Prayers in a Hospital Room*

"Dear Heavenly Father, we are grateful for this hospital, the doctors and nurses and for all who help us when we are ill. We are most grateful for Jesus, the great physician, who is concerned with all our diseases. We are thankful for him and his promise to be with us always. We ask your help for this patient, to comfort, strengthen and bring him to his normal state of health. Be with his loved ones while he is away. Watch over us all and help us to be like Jesus. In his name. Amen."

—Howard Swenney

Father in Heaven, I approach thy throne of grace and mercy in behalf of this precious friend. I come with reverence, but also with boldness, praying through Jesus who knew suffering, pain and all kinds of trouble. I pray that you will help Mrs._____ to get well, if it be in keeping with thy righteous will. May she get well soon.

Bless those who are seeing after her, and please guide the hand of the surgeon when Mrs. _____ goes into surgery tomorrow morning. Will you give her the patience she needs during these days of illness. Bless her loved ones also, those who are at home and those who are away. Help us all, Father, to be strong and healthy spiritually, most of all. In the loving name of Jesus. Amen.


(Note: The second one is an example of a prayer beside the bed of one who is, or may be, unsaved.)

# CHAPTER EIGHT

# These Things Will Cause You to Pray More and Pray Better

You will find yourself praying more often and with greater enjoyment and satisfaction, if you will give attention to the things suggested in this chapter.

## Cultivate an Acquaintance With God

Become acquainted with the Lord and cultivate that acquaintance. The Bible, which reveals God to you also helps you to cultivate a personal relationship with him. Daily Bible study; serious Bible study. This is what you need. Also you need both private and public worship. Put family worship in your daily schedule and decide you will not miss any assembly of the church for public worship. Commit yourself to the work of soul-winning. Involve yourself in evangelism, both local and world-wide. When you do this you will start praying more.

These things will make it easier for you to live the Christian life and will cause you to pray more and to pray better: *(1)* daily Bible study, *(2)* the practice of regular worship, *(3)* taking part as well as attending church services, and *(4)* the work of soul-winning.

## Be Conscious of These Four Things

Come to understand, then remember, the Lord is real, the Lord is near, the Lord is great, and the Lord is good.

*1. God is real.* This universe did not just happen. Neither did you. Only the fool says in his heart, There is no God

(Psalms 53:1). The Psalmist made this confession: "Lord, thou hast been our dwelling place in all generations. Before the mountains were brought forth, or ever thou hadst formed the earth and the world, even from everlasting to everlasting, thou art God." (Psalms 90:1, 2).

You know all these things. But, does the Lord seem as real to you as he ought? God must have been very real to the boy Joseph. When under the extreme pressure of temptation, he reacted by saying, "How then can I do this great wickedness, and sin against God?" (Genesis 39:9). To the early church, the Lord was real; for they walked in the fear of the Lord (Acts 9:31).

Understand and remember that the Lord is real.

2. *God is near.* Know this. Remember this. As Paul said in Athens long ago, "He is not far from every one of us: for in him we live, and move, and have our being." (Acts 17:27, 28).

The Psalmist asks, "Whither shall I go from thy Spirit? Or whither shall I flee from thy presence? If I ascend up into heaven, thou art there: if I make my bed in hell, behold, thou art there. If I take the wings of the morning, and dwell in the uttermost parts of the sea; even there shall thy hand lead me, and thy right hand shall hold me" (Psalms 139:7-10). Yes, the Lord is near. You can draw near to God and he will draw near to you (James 4:8). As you endeavor to execute the great commission, you go out with the promise of Christ, "Lo, I am with you always, even unto the end of the world" (Matthew 28:20). Where two or three of you meet together in the Lord's name, there is he in the midst of you (Matthew 18:20). You are promised in John 14:23 that the Father and the Son abide in you, because you love Jesus and keep his words. Paul tells you in 1 Corinthians 6:19 that your body is the temple of the Holy Spirit which is in you.

The presence of a good man exerts a valuable influence on people. I saw a group of men standing around talking and using vile language. Then a good man walked up. As soon as they recognized him, they stopped using ugly words. Incidents like this happen all the time. But, people must realize the good man is present if he is to exert an influence. So it is in the spiritual realm. The Lord is not far from everyone, but only those who realize it are influenced for good. Know and remember that God is near. He is near all the time.

*3.   God is great.* If you know this and remember it, you will pray more. You will pray better.

Nebuchadnezzar had this fact impressed upon him. He said of God, "He doeth according to his will in the armies of heaven, and among the inhabitants of the earth: none can stay his hand, or say unto him, What doest thou?" (Daniel 4:35). God is great.

Israel was told that when God was with them they would be able to put to flight their enemies. Moses said, "One of you shall chase a hundred, and a hundred of you shall chase ten thousand" (Leviticus 26:7, 8). I love the statement which John made to us, "Ye are of God, little children, and have overcome them: because greater is he that is in you, than he that is in the world" (1 John 4:4). "O Lord, my God, how great thou art!"

You know the Lord is strong and able to save you to the uttermost. You also know he is your judge, and one day you shall stand before him to give account of the deeds done in the body, according to what you have done, whether it be good or bad. (Hebrews 9:27; 2 Corinthians 5:10).

Know and remember that God is great. Trust him. Rely upon him. Also, serve him with reverence and godly fear. If you do this, you will be a praying man.

God is full of mercy, "Jehovah is merciful and gracious, slow to anger and abundant in lovingkindness" (Psalms 103:8). God is good; and the things he requires of you and the restrictions he places upon you are all for your good. As it is said in Deuteronomy 6:24, "And the Lord commanded us to do all these statutes, to fear the Lord our God, for our good always." In every temptation, the Lord makes a way of escape, and doesn't suffer you to be tempted above your ability (1 Corinthians 10:13). He causes all things to work together for your good (Romans 8:28). It was because of God's goodness, that John could say, "And this is the confidence that we have in him, that, if we ask anything according to his will, he heareth us" (1 John 5:14).

When you realize God is good and is the giver of every good and perfect gift (James 1:17), your heart is thankful; and it is natural for you to pray.

So, "Anchor your soul in this, that God is good." Young man or young lady, when you go out from your father's home into the world, make sure your soul is anchored in this fact. Whatever happens to you, for good or for ill, just remember that God is good. You may not understand why things are happening as they are, but let this be your anchor. This will keep you from bitterness, despondency, fear, hatred, hopelessness. This will make a prayerful person of you.

4. *The Lord is good.* He is the holy God (Joshua 24:19). It is impossible for God to lie (Titus 1:2). God cannot be tempted with evil; neither tempteth he any man (James 1:13).

## Know Thyself

It will help you in your prayer life to know yourself.

1. *Know about your dignity and worth.* You are made in the very image of God (Genesis 1:26). You are above the beasts of the field. As David said about the exalted position

God has given to man, "For thou hast made him a little lower than the angels, and hast crowned him with glory and honor. Thou madest him to have dominion over the works of thy hands; thou hast put all things under his feet" (Psalms 8:5, 6).

Know that you have a never-dying soul. Listen to what Jesus said, "He that believeth on me, though he were dead, yet shall he live: And whosoever liveth and believeth in me shall never die" (John 11:25, 26). Actually, you are a spiritual being, tabernacling in a body of flesh (2 Corinthians 5:1). This should make you see that your greatest need is not for something material, but for God's spiritual blessings which are in Christ Jesus.

2. *Know that this world is not your home.* You are just a pilgrim here. "For we know that if our earthly house of this tabernacle were dissolved, we have a building of God, a house not made with hands, eternal in the heavens" (2 Corinthians 5:1). Knowing this will help you to obey Paul's charge, "Set your affections on things above, not on things of the earth" (Colossians 3:2). It will help you to know better how to pray. It will also make you more grateful so that you will pray more.

3. *Know that you are human.* The Psalmist prayed, "Put them in fear, O Lord: that the nations may know themselves to be but men" (Psalms 9:20). When his brothers spoke to Joseph about taking vengeance, he asked, "Am I in the place of God?" (Genesis 50:19). Once when King Herod made an oration, the people shouted, This is the voice of a god, and not of a man. Then an angel of the Lord smote Herod because he failed to give God the glory, and he was eaten of worms and gave up the ghost. See Acts 12:21-23.

Haughtiness is inexcusable. "He hath shewed thee, O man, what is good; and what doth the Lord require of thee, but to do justly, and to love mercy, and to walk humbly with thy God" (Micah 6:8).

*4. Know, not only that you are human, but that you are unworthy before God.* "We have before proved both Jews and Gentiles, that they are all under sin; as it is written, There is none righteous, no, not one . . . that every mouth may be stopped, and all the world become guilty before God . . . For all have sinned, and come short of the glory of God" (Romans 3:10-23). Man is a sinner. He cannot earn salvation. He cannot atone for his own sins. Man has to do as he is told in Isaiah 45:22: "Look unto me, and be ye saved, all the ends of the earth: for I am God and there is none else." If you get to heaven, it will be by God's grace. Even concerning the blessings of this earth, you should have the attitude of Jacob, who prayed and said, "I am not worthy of the least of all the mercies, and of all the truth, which thou has shewed unto thy servant" (Genesis 32:10).

Know that you are a man, not a god.

*5. Know also that you are a dependent.* You depend on the good Lord for life, breath and all things. You need to pray, "Give us this day our daily bread." Whether it be a physical need or a spiritual one, you must look to the Lord for it. As Jesus said, "Without me ye can do nothing" (John 15:5). On the other hand, Paul was able to say, "I can do all things through Christ which strengtheneth me" (Phil. 4:13). It is no wonder Paul was such a praying man and often asked the brethren to pray for him. If you know how dependent you are, you will be a praying person too.

## Summary

Would you like to be a prayerful person? Would you like to pray better? Give serious attention to these things:

I. Cultivate an acquaintance with your Lord.

II. Be conscious of these four things:

    1. God is real.

    2. God is near.

    3. God is great.

    4. God is good.

III. Know yourself.

    1. Know you dignity and worth.

    2. Know that this world is not your home.

    3. Know that you are human.

    4. Know that you are unworthy before God.

    5. Know that you are dependent upon God.

Some one has said, "The one concern of the devil is to keep Christians from praying. He fears nothing from prayerless studies, prayerless work, prayerless religion. He laughs at our toil, mocks at our wisdom, but trembles when we pray."

## *What Now?*

You have not graduated from the subject, How to Pray. You never will.

At this point you should have studied this book, chapter by chapter, making markings in it, and doing the exercises. Now:

*1.* If you have not already done so, start immediately practicing what you have learned. Pray at home. Let the proper people know you are ready to lead a short prayer in public, so that you will be called on. It is very important that you apply what you have learned.

2.   Re-read this book about 4 to 6 weeks from now.

3.   Keep the book on your reading table, and pick it up occasionally to review certain parts. Check the index, or thumb through the book, and re-read the things of interest.

4.   After you have led a prayer, it will be good to review pertinent portions of the book, to see how you can improve on the way you prayed.

5.   Keep praying and keep asking the Lord to help you with your prayers.